Art of
Corporate Communication

Published by :
Lotus Press Publishers & Distributors

Art of
Corporate Communication

A.K. Banerjee

4735/22, Prakash Deep Building
Ansari Road, Darya Ganj,
New Delhi - 110002

Lotus Press : Publishers & Distributors
Unit No. 220, 2nd Floor, 4735/22, Prakash Deep Building,
Ansari Road, Darya Ganj, New Delhi- 110002
Ph.: 41325510, 98118-38000
• E-mail : lotuspress1984@gmail.com
www.lotuspress.co.in

Art of Corporate Communication

ISBN: 978-81-8382-211-4

Printed & Published by : **Lotus Press Publishers & Distributors,** New Delhi-02

PREFACE

The corporate communication today is an indispensable component of any organisation, whether it is at the personal, group or complete organisational level. In a world mediated by the information meted out through various communication channels, communication is the most essential medium which can bring in changes indispensable to an 'organisation or enterprise. As any responsible and sharp leader of an enterprise would know, effective communication is not only crucial to the efficiency of the organisation, but should be actively fostered so as to enhance productivity and profit.

The present text has been designed to communicate readers about what entails the art of corporate communication in the contemporary scenario, particularly the socio-economic and cultúral changes that it is informed by, and what it means to be a skilled communicator. Focussing on all types of communication modes and channels, whether verbal or otherwise, the book is a handy referral that seeks to ensure that the readers have a clear idea of what it takes to put across information to the other side in a manner which not only ensures the clarity of the communication, but also the execution of it. It is hoped that the incisive content of the book is appreciated by all. Any suggestions for further improvement are most welcome.

Editor

Other Books on

MANAGEMENT BOOKS

1. Be A Better Project Manager **(New)**
2. Be A Better Problem Solver **(New)**
3. Be A Better Motivator **(New)**
4. Be A Better Time Manager **(New)**
5. Effective Director **(New)**
6. Network Marketing **(New)**
7. Art of Entrepreneurship **(New)**
8. How to Beat Your Competitors **(New)**
9. How to Negotiate Effectively **(New)**
10. Make Your Boss Happy **(New)**
11. Art of Advertising
12. Art of Marketing
13. Art of Growing Business
14. Art of Retailing
15. Art of Leadership
16. Art of Team Building
17. Art of Corporate Communication
18. Art of Organisational Management
19. Improve Your Marketing and Grow Your Business
20. What Customers Really Want
21. Effective Presentation
22. The Right Decision Every Time
23. Develop Your Decision Making Skills
24. Develop Your Team Building Skills
25. Develop Your Skills to Conduct Effective Meetings
26. How to Export and Import
27. How to Use Money
28. How to Start My Business
29. How to Organise My Office
30. How to Manufacture My Products
31. How to Promote and Advertise
32. How to Sell My Products
33. How to Develop and Maintain Quality

Unit No. 220, Second Floor, 4735/22,
Prakash Deep Building, Ansari Road, Darya Ganj,
New Delhi - 110002, Ph.: 23280047, 09811838000
E-mail: lotuspress1984@gmail.com, www.lotuspress.co.in

CONTENTS

1

THE ART OF CORPORATE COMMUNICATION

"Communication" is a process — an activity that serves to connect senders and receivers of messages through space and time. Although human beings tend to be interested primarily in the study of human communication, the process is present in all living things and, it can be argued, in all things.

The word "communicate" derives from the word "common"— to share, exchange, send along, transmit, talk, gesture, write, put in use, relate. So an investigation of this subject might begin with the question: What do all studies of communication have in common? What are the shared concepts that make the study of "communication" different from the study of subjects such as "thought" or "literature" or "life?" When someone says, "this is a communication problem," what does that mean?

When a baby sees his mother's face for the first time, communication happens. When someone steps out onto a beach in Goa and water touches his feet communication happens. When the Indian parliament passes a new bill to curb monopolies in the market and the President signs, communication happens. When a computer in New Delhi calls up a computer in Tokyo in Japan and transmits a message, communication happens.

Communication is a general phenomenon. It occurs in nature, wherever life exists. Whether we recognise it or not, we have no choice but to communicate. If we try to avoid communicating by not replying to messages, we are nevertheless sending a message, but it may not be the one we want or intend. When we don't say yes, we may be saying no by default – and vice-versa. The only choice we can make about communication is whether we are going to attempt to communicate effectively. What do we mean by communicating effectively? The object of communication is to convey thoughts/ intentions/ emotions/ facts/ideas of one person or group to the others. When the message sent is received and understood by the receiver in the same sense, as the sender wants to convey, effective communication takes place. When the receiver misunderstands a message we consider it a distortion in communication. Throughout our study, we would try to improve our communication skills so that we can make ourselves better understood in our communications.

The fact is that we spend so much of our time in communicating; we tend to assume that we are experts. Surveys indicate that when business professionals are asked to rate their communication skills, virtually everyone overestimates his or her abilities as a communicator. There is a natural tendency to blame the other person for the problems in understanding or making ourselves understood. The better option is to improve one's own communication. One has to be always on a look to identify his weak points as a communicator and strive to overcome them. This needs thorough understanding of meaning and process of communication.

MEANING OF COMMUNICATION

Communication is derived from the Latin word

'communis', which means, "to share" that is, sharing of ideas, concepts, feelings and emotions. The science of communication is almost as old as man himself. Form time immemorial; the need to share or to communicate had been felt. Different vehicles/channels were identified and subsequently improvised for the purpose of transmission of ideas and concepts. A study of these channels enables us to gain an insight into the process of communication.

The importance of communication can be gauged from the fact that we are communicating in some form or the other almost every moment of our lives. Whether we are walking, talking, playing, sitting, or even sleeping, a message is being formulated and transmitted. Man, who is a social animal, is constantly interacting with other individuals. For him it is necessary to understand the art of communication and apply or modify it in a suitable manner. Man possesses the ability to communicate, which is much more than a composition of certain symbolise or to understand concepts in terms of images or symbols. It is this ability that helps him to communicate. Communication then, it may be stated, is much more than an understanding of the spoken or written language. It is a composite of symbols, gestures, and illustrations that accompany either the spoken or the written word.

PURPOSE OF COMMUNICATION

People in organisations typically spend over 75% of their time in an interpersonal situation; thus it is no surprise to find that at the root of a large number of organisational problems is poor communications. Effective communication is an essential component of organisational success whether it is at the interpersonal, intergroup, intragroup, organisational, or external levels.

In the business situation of a manager, as he goes higher up in the hierarchy is to coordinate, issue instructions, collate information, and then present it. All these activities require effective communication skills the sooner these skills are honed, the easier it is for the manager to accomplish tasks. Similar is the case of the junior manager vying for a quick promotion. As work in the organisation is always done in conjunction with other people, effective communication skills become a necessity. Let us compare the progression of two junior managers up the ladder of success possessing almost the same academic qualifications and almost similar personality traits. Only one of them would be able to make it to the Managing Director's chair. Without doubt it would be the candidate with excellent communication skills.

Prior to entry in any organisation, certain communicative abilities are also looked for in candidates. Ability to speak, conduct oneself properly in an interview, get along with others, listen carefully and accurately, make effective presentations, prepare good yet brief report, make proposals, sell ideas, convince and persuade others are some of the attributes looked for in a candidate. If an individual possesses these attributes looked for in a candidate. If an individual possesses these attributes or can train himself to excel in them, he himself would realise how much easier it is for him only to secure a comfortable position in an organisation but also to achieve success.

COMMUNICATION PROCESS

Communication is a process that serves to connect senders and receivers of messages in space and time. Although human beings tend to be interested primarily in the study of human communication, the process is present in all living things and, it can be argued, in all things. From this we may conclude that communication is a fundamental, universal process.

Self and Society

Messages are formed in the mind of one individual and interpreted in the mind of another. Yet the formation and interpretation of messages are affected by the groups to which the individuals belong. Thus, a complete understanding of human communication must take into account both human psychology and human social interaction.

Information

To receive messages human beings must make use of their senses. However, the senses continually process large volumes of data, not all of which are the result of communication. It is the human ability to discern, recognise, and remember patterns in this constant flow of data that makes meaningful communication possible.

Signs and Language

Some patterns of data bring to mind memories of previous patterns. These "signs," as they are called, can be assembled into large, powerful patterns called "languages." Much of human communication is carried on through the use of language.

Interaction and Relationships

In face-to-face situations human beings cannot avoid communicating with one another. This "interpersonal" communication, which involves processes such as "speech" and "body language," plays an important role in the formation, development, and dissolution of human relationships.

Mass Communication

Approximately five hundred years ago a new form of communication arose. This "mass" communication process, which makes use of permanent text that can be made available to millions of people at the same time, has quickly become an important factor in the lives of many human beings.

COMMUNICATION ENVIRONMENT

Human communication takes place within, and cannot be separated from, the complex social environments within which all communicators must live. Systems of belief, technological media, and the presence of cultural artifacts all affect the communication process and contribute to the development of the human social reality.

Systems

A "system" is typically described as a collection of parts which are interconnected, or related to, one another and which also relate to the environment which surrounds the system.

To say that the elements of a system are interconnected implies that if something happens to change one part, then at least one other part must change, too. Naturally, as soon as that second part changes, some other part must then change ... and so on. This is somewhat like the effect of touching a bowl of gelatin — a single touch results in a long period of jiggling motion. Because systems interact with their environments, they are constantly being "touched" from the outside. This means that most systems are constantly changing, and, because these changes take time, a system cannot be described as having one particular shape. It is this property that makes systems useful for studying the kinds of situations that scholars usually refer to as events, or processes.

The idea of a system is well illustrated by the device called a "mobile." The parts of this system, or objects, as they are often called, "fishes." The relationships are established by the bars, which maintain a horizontal spacing among the fish, and the pieces of string, which keep the fish at certain vertical depths. Notice that the strings and bars

— Connect every fish with every other fish,

— Allow the fish to move around quite a bit, yet confine them to a certain area and keep them from falling apart.

This is a fine example of how a system works. If any one fish moves, at least one other fish will react by moving, too. Thus, the smallest breeze will keep the mobile in constant motion. From the simplest perspective, a system can be said to consist of four things.

— The first is objects. The objects are the parts, elements, or variables of the system. These objects may be physical or abstract or both, depending on the nature of the system.

— Second, a system consists of attributes, or the qualities or properties of the system and its objects.

— Third, a system must possess internal relationships among its objects. This characteristic is a crucial defining quality of systems. A relationship among objects implies a mutual effect and constraint.

— Fourth, systems also possess an environment. They do not exist in a vacuum but are affected by their surroundings.

Clearly, the "fish" mobile meets these requirements.

It is important to do the following exercise. Thinking about systems in this way is the most effective way to understand them. Consider each of the three systems named here and try to:

- Name some of the objects that make up the system,
- Name some of the relationships among the objects,
- Describe the environment of the system, and
- Describe ways in which the system is constantly changing.

Communication Connects

But communication is not merely passive connection. Rather, communication is the process of connecting. It is a collection of renewable actions that work throughout space and over time to form relationships among objects. Communication is not an object itself; it is not a thing, and this leads to a second insight into the nature of communication.

Communication Happens

This is an important observation. It implies that communication can never fully be understand by looking only at "things." To understand communication, we must also look at the relationships among the "things" and at the environments in which the "things" reside.

STAGES IN COMMUNICATION CYCLE

Communication is a two-way process in which there is an exchange and progression of ideas towards a mutually accepted direction or goal. For this process to materialise, it is essential that the basic elements of communication be identified. These elements are:

Sender/ Encoder/ Speaker

The person who initiates the communication process is normally referred to as the sender. From his personal data bank he selects ideas, encodes and finally transits them to the receiver. The entire burden of communication then rests upon the sender or encoder. His choice of images and words the combination of the two is what goads the receiver to listen carefully. In this process a number of factors come into play, primary among them being an understanding of the recipient and his needs. If the message can be formulated in accordance with the expectations of the receiver, the level of acceptance is going to be higher. For example, a consultant wishes to communicate with the HRD manager of a company. The objective is to secure consultancy projects on training-of personnel. If the consultant wishes the HRD manager to communicate with him, he has to ensure that their goals converge. He has a tough task ahead of him. The manager had been interacting with many consultants. Why should he pay heed to the proposal of this consultant? In a situation such as this, a good strategy to be adopted is to expand the purview of the proposal and make it company specific. The result could be highlighted and spelt out in terms of increase in sales. If sufficient preparation has been done, the message too would increase in sales. If sufficient preparation has been done, the message too would be formulated in a manner conducive to the interests of the HRD manager.

Receiver/ Decoder/ Listener

The listener receives an encoded message, which he attempts to decode. This process is carried on in relation to the work environment and the value perceived in terms of the work situation. If the goal of the sender is envisioned as similar to his own, the listener becomes more receptive. The decoding of the message is done in almost entirely the same terms as were intended by the sender. In the example cited above, as soon as the HRD manager realises that the proposal of the consultant is going to result in tangible benefits, he becomes more receptive and his interest in communication is reinforced.

Message

Message is the encoded idea transmitted by the sender. The formulation of the message is very important, for a message, which is incorrectly structured, can turn the receiver hostile or make him lose interest. At this stage the sender has to be extremely cautious. What is the order in which he would like to present his ideas? Suppose he has four points to make would he *(a)* move in the stereotyped manner of presenting them in a sequence or *(b)* would he like to be innovative and proceed in a creative way? Probability is high that in case *(a)* he might become monotonous and in case *(b)* he might touch a wrong spot. How then should the message be formulated and transmitted? The ordering, as stated earlier, should be based on the requirements of the listener so that its significance is immediately grasped. The minute the receiver finds his goals codified in the message, he sits up, listens and responds. The message thus has made an impact.

Medium

Another important element of communication is the medium or channel. It could be oral, written or non-verbal. Prior to the composition of the message, the medium/channel should be decided. Each medium follows its own set of rules and regulations. For example, in oral communication one can afford to be a little informal, but when using the written mode, all rules of communication need to be observed. It must be remembered that anything in writing is a document that would be filed for records or circulated to all concerned.

Feedback

This is the most important component of

communication. Effective communication takes place only when there is feedback. The errors and flaws that abound in business situations are a result of lack of feedback. Let us take a look at the typical responses of people involved in miscommunication: "This is not what I meant" or "This is not what I said", or "This was not my intention". If feedback is solicited on all occasions, this error can be minimised or even completely done away with. Fallacious statements or erroneous conclusions are made because of lack of confirmation through feedback and discrepancy between the message transmitted and understood.

Activity

Try not to narrate a story of a film you recently saw to your friend. Ask your friend to tell the story, which you have just told him.

BARRIERS TO EFFECTIVE COMMUNICATION

There are a wide number of sources of noise or interference that can enter into the communication process. This can occur when people now each other very well and should understand the sources of error. In a work setting, it is even more common since interactions involve people who not only don't have years of experience with each other, but communication is complicated by the complex and often conflictual relationships that exist at work. In a work setting, the following suggests a number of sources of noise:

- *Language:* The choice of words or language in which a sender encodes a message will influence the quality of communication. Because language is a symbolic representation of a phenomenon, room for interpreation and distortion of the meaning exists.

- Defensiveness, distorted perceptions, guilt, project, transference, distortions from the past.
- Misreading of body language, tone and other non-verbal forms of communication.
- Noisy transmission.
- Receiver distortion: selective hearing, ignoring non-verbal cues.
- Power struggles.
- Self-fulfiling assupmtions.
- Language-different levels of meaning.
- Managers hesitation to be candid.
- Assumptions—e.g. assuming others see situation same as you, has same feelings as you.
- Distrusted source, erroneous translation, value judgement, state of mind of two people.
- *Perceptual biases:* People attend to stimuli in the environment in very different ways. We each have shortcuts that we use to organise data. Invariably, these shortcuts introduce some biases into communication. Some of these shortcuts include stereotyping, projection, and self-fulfilling prophecies. Stereotyping is one of the most common. This is when we assume that the other person has certain characteristics based on the group to which they belong without validating that they in fact have these characteristics.
- *Interpersonal relationships:* How we perceive communication is affected by the past experience with the individual. Percpetion is also affected by the organisational relationship two people have. For example, communication from a superior may be perceived differently than that from a subordinate or peer.

- *Cultural differences:* Effective communication requires deciphering the basic values, motives, aspirations, and assumptions that operate across geographical lines. Given some dramatic differences across cultures in approaches to such areas as time, space, and privacy, the opportunities for mis-communication while we are in cross-cultural situations are plentiful.

TOWARDS EFFECTIVE COMMUNICATION

Over 70% of our time is spent communicating with others, and that's the one interaction every person must do. Everyone must communicate their needs and ideas. Every organisation must communicate its products and services. Unfortunately, many people have trouble in this area. Some just don't have the professional impact they need to get ahead in today's corporate world. Communication is just as important as what we say because people judge us, our companies, our products, our services, and our professionalism by the way we write, act, dress, talk, and manage our responsibilities. In short, how well we communicate with others.

Successful people know how to communicate for results. They know how to say what they mean and get what they want without hurting the people they deal with. You deal daily with peers, outside groups, customers, employees, and managers, and you must have a good communication style.

When we ask people how well they communicate, their answers usually fall into one of three categories. First, and most prevalent, is the person who responds, "I communicate perfectly. I spell everything out so there's nothing left to doubt."

Another will react with surprise and ask me, "What do you mean 'how well?' I don't think about communicating, I just do it."

The third type will reflect on the question thoughtfully before saying something like, "How can one ever know how well they get their ideas across to another person? All I can tell you is I work more hours trying to communicate than I can count, and it still doesn't work some of the time." Each answer, in its own way, is correct.

Communicating today is both a discipline and a liberation. Our language is flexible; one size fits all. It's a language in which ravel and unravel mean the same thing; flammable and inflammable mean the same thing; fat chance, slim chance, no chance at all mean the same thing. Communication is both a science and a feeling; it's often a cinch, and often an impossibility.

The smell of a woman's perfume, the taste of semisweet chocolate, the sight of a blind person's cane, the feel of the feverish brow of a sick child, the sound of the background music of a horror movie—all these move us to action or reaction. These are all examples of effective communication, and none of them involve words.

Communication is full of risks; despite whatever precautions and plans we make, we can never really be sure of our success. No communication ever travels from sender to receiver in the same shape intended by the sender. And, no matter how hard you try, the message will never be what you say—the message is always what they hear. But if you have a system to go by, you can at least reduce the risk and improve your chance of being effective.

For communication to occur, there must be a two-way interchange of feelings, ideas, values; clarification of signals; and a fine-tuning of skills.

Adjust the Climate

Whenever people get together to communicate with one

another, two factors are always present. First, there is some sort of content to be covered—instructions, news, gossip, ideas, reports, evaluations, etc.

All of us are familiar with the content of communication, because it's the most obvious factor, and because we deal with it every day. The second factor that is always present when people get together to communicate is the atmosphere or feeling that accompanies what you say. This is known as the communication climate.

Physical climate affects us in many ways. When it's cold, we wear warm clothes. When it's raining, we wear protective clothes. And it's not uncommon for weather conditions to affect our mood. Communication climates also affect us. They can be either positive or negative. When the communication climate is positive, it's easier for us to communicate, solve problems, reach decisions, express thoughts and feelings. In short, it makes working and dealing with other people more pleasant and productive. We've all been in restaurants, stores, offices, and homes where we felt comfortable and at ease. We usually want to go back to those places. We've also been in homes, offices, and shops where the climate has been negative. In those instances, we were uncomfortable, uneasy, and less open. We usually don't enjoy attempting to communicate or do business in a negative climate. Are you making the climate negative for those you work with?

Choose Your Channel

Like a radio, human transmitters and receivers have channels. A communication channel is the medium through which information passes from sender to receiver: lecture, written messages, telephone conversations, face-to-face dialogue, and group meetings.

The choice of a channel may affect the quality of the communication and, in turn, the degree to which the receiver will respond to it. Therefore, you must decide which channel will be most effective in accomplishing your purpose.

Written communication should be used when communicating complex facts and figures or information, such as engineering, legal or financial data, since communication breakdowns often result when complex material is presented orally. Written communication is also the best channel when communicating with large numbers of people, when transmitting large amounts of data, or when you need a record of the communication.

The telephone is appropriate when communicating simple facts to a few people. The phone also has more impact and sense of urgency than written communication, but not as much as a meeting. To insure that messages are understood on the phone, you may want to ask for feedback and check to make sure the communication link is complete.

Face-to-face communication has more urgency than meetings. It also has the advantage of speed, allows considerable two-way communication to take place, and usually elicits a quick response. It's usually best to use face-to-face dialogue when the interaction is personal—when giving praise, counselling, or taking disciplinary action.

Meetings are appropriate when there is a need for verbal interaction among members of a group. Studies have revealed that supervisors spend more than half of their potential productive time in meetings, discussions, and conferences. For this reason, it's important to decide in advance whether a meeting will actually achieve the desired result.

Eliminate Static

Another helpful skill is elimination of communication "static" or barriers. If there's too much static, or noise, there's a garbled message. The problem is that each of us has different barriers, and we don't usually know what kind of noise the other person is hearing. Sometimes we guess, and sometimes we guess wrong. The major barrier to communication is our natural tendency to judge, evaluate, approve, or disapprove the other person's statements.

Suppose the person next to you at lunch today says, "I really like what Kay duPont has to say." What will you say? Your reply will probably be either approval or disapproval of the attitude expressed. You'll either say, "I do too!" or you'll say, "I think she's terrible." In other words, your first reaction will be to evaluate it from your point of view, and approve or disapprove what the other person said. Although the tendency to make evaluations is common in almost all conversation, it is very much heightened in those situations where feelings and emotions are involved.

Tune in

One of the best ways to "tune in" to the other person is to find out how they process and store the information they receive. Studies of Neurolinguistic Programming (NLP) have proved that there are three sensory process types: Visual, Auditory, and Kinesthetic.

Some people are visually oriented. They remember and imagine things by what they look like. They store pictures. Some people are auditory—they store sounds. Some people are kinesthetic—they store touch sensations.

How can you figure out a person's processing system? By listening. People tend to broadcast how they process information, how they file their data. Visually oriented people say things like: "Here's what it looks like to me. Do you see what I mean? Do you get the picture? I need a clearer vision of that. That's not coming in clear to me." All visually oriented terms.

Auditory people remember and imagine things by what they sound like. They say: "Here's what it sounds like to me. That rings a bell. Do you hear what I mean? We need to have more harmony in this office. We're not in tune on this." Kinesthetic people remember and imagine things by the feel of them. They say: "Here's what it feels like to me. Do you grasp what I'm saying? That was a rough problem. That was a heavy burden. That was a weighty issue."

People don't always use the same sensory words, of course, but we do tend to use one sensory process about 70% of the time. If you want me to understand how you feel or see what you mean or get in tune with your ideas, you need to talk to me in words I'll relate to—either visual, auditory, or kinesthetic. If you talk to me in flowers, and I hear in pastry, we can't communicate. This is a very sophisticated form of communicating, and can be very effective.

Know Your Non-verbals

Body movement, eye contact, posture, and clothing are also very important elements. In fact, studies prove that 93% of your message is nonverbal and symbolic. Employees learn to cue on the boss' moods, spouses learn to react to each other's movements, children instinctively watch for signs from their parents.

Studies have also taught us that sometimes our tongues say one thing, our bodies say another thing, and our symbols—like clothing and hairstyles—say still a third thing.

2

ORAL COMMUNICATION SKILLS

Conversation is so basic to human existence that any study of it inevitably leads to some of life's most important rules—rules that lead to trouble if ignored. Consider the following list of consequences of poor conversation skills.

Ask yourself if any of these basic emotions and conditions is a persistent part of your social and business life:

Disrespect	Embarrassment
rejection	exhaustion
frustration	failure
anger	fear
being misunderstood	humiliation
being misinterpreted	loneliness
depression	powerlessness
giving offense	weakness
being insulted	being overlooked
disappointment	impatience

Good conversation skills, on the other hand, lead to success, and success leads to more success. Good verbal abilities usually promote good relations with others, influence, respect, and a reputation for leadership and effectiveness. People with these advantages go through life feeling the emotions and talents listed below.

stimulated	empowered
energised	vital
passionate	centred
motivated	respected
excited	well-liked
challenged	included
determined	focused
flexible	fortunate
contributing	rewarded
effective	in control
comfortable	satisfied
confident	lucky
resourceful	positive

Society's rules aren't always obvious. The rules that allow us to get by and survive are fairly simple (don't run red lights, don't make bank robbery a career). But other rules, the ones that confer real success, not mere survival, can sometimes be as difficult to detect as black holes in deep space.

When your career progress bogs down, when your relationships are weak or troubled, when you have a hard time making friends, when you have difficulty making yourself heard, and when people take advantage of you, it is because you have an imperfect comprehension of those shadowy rules that allow you to focus social power to your advantage.

No one in our world succeeds strictly on his or her own. True accomplishment requires that you efficiently influence those around you in positive ways. The primary tool of influence is communication, and like society itself, communication has rules that few fully understand.

FEATURES OF ORAL COMMUNICATION

Communication is a composite of speaking and listening. Honing skills in both these areas is absolutely essential if the communicator wishes to impress the receiver. The initial impact is made by speaking abilities of the sender. Equally important is the ability to listen carefully. If the overall effectiveness of these two components is considered. It would be seen that he ability to listen rather than to speak fluently impress more. The two activities viz, speaking and listening, cannot be segregated. Both are closely intertwined an overall impact is created if both these skills are used effectively. Let us use the word 'IMPRESS' as an acronym to understand the basic features of communication or concept, which, if once understood, would define helps us to impress the other person.

I – Idea

The first step in the process of communication is to decide on the idea which needs to be communicated. There may be a host of ideas passing through the mind of the sender. Depending upon the situation and the receiver, the speaker selects the idea suited to the occasion.

M – Message

Once the idea has been selected, it needs to be clothed in a language that is comprehensible to the receiver. The encoding of the message has to be done keeping a number of factors in mind. What is it that needs to be stated? What is the language that is going to be understood by the receiver? Does the idea necessarily pertain to the interest of the receiver? What is it that the receiver actually needs to know? Framing of the message, if done (keeping answers to these question in mind), would definitely make an impact on the receiver.

P - Pause/ Paragraphs

The significance of pauses cannot be underestimated. Pauses should be juxtaposed at just the right minute so that the receiver can assimilate the impact of the message. The use of pauses would be best understood in the context of a presentation. The presenter should, at the time of making a presentation, use this device suitably. Excessive usage of this device can lead the presentation into being one that is pretty boring and monotonous. The right use of pauses actually stimulates the audience. The impact is often so great and forceful that the receiver actually leans forward in their chairs when the presenter pauses, as if urging him to resume the presentation. This device, in the course of the interaction, lasts for barely a few seconds. However, the impact is long and meaningful. In written communication pauses get translated into paragraphs. If the decision to use a certain number of paragraphs is right and the division of points in these paragraphs is also correct, then written communication becomes meaningful and creates a positive impression.

R - Receiver

The receiver is the most important person in the process of communication who could, if he so desires, also prove to be the most difficult. He is the one who is generally led into the interaction. In order to draw his attention, it is imperative that there be an extra plus that would retain his interest and make him attentive to the ensuing communication. To satisfy this criterion the sender should address himself to the needs and expectations of the receiver. Formulating the statements according to a mutually accepted goal is a good way of proceeding and drawing his attention.

E - Empathy

In communication empathy should be used to help us understand the other individual, the strategies that he adopts and the responses that he gives at a particular moment. It would be worthwhile to note that all communication is situation bound. The same individual in two different situations might use the same words but his intention might be totally different. Gauging the exact meaning of an utterance can only be done when we literally put ourselves in the shoes of the other person and try to understand the situation from the perspective of the sender.

Each individual, as a sender has, what we refer to as, a 'logic bubble' that enables him to formulate his message in a particular fashion. The same holds true for the receiver or the listener. The greater the *empathy* between them, the higher the level of understanding and more the receptivity to messages word, namely, "sympathy", which is different in connotation. Sympathy is placing the sender on a higher pedestal and viewing the other in a sympathetic light.

S - Sender

The communication process hinges on the sender. He initiates the interaction and comes up with ideas and concepts that he wishes to share with the receiver. His role is the most crucial. The success or failure of interaction depends on him and on the strategies he adopts to get his message across by securing the attention of the receiver. A cautious sender would understand that there is a difference between the mental frames of the participants. Such a difference could be a result of discrepancy in interpretation of words, perception of reality, and attitudes, opinions and emotions. Message, if formulated, with awareness along these areas, is sure to bring success to the sender.

S - Security Check

Effective communication necessitates that the receiver listens carefully to the utterances of the sender so that the end results are positive. The primary rule is: *never be in - a rush to commence communication.* Sufficient time and effort should be put in formulating the message. Suppose the sender wishes to communicate five points. The sequencing and necessary substantiation of points with facts and figures should be done prior to the actual beginning of the communication process. This would build confidence in the message and eliminate possibility of errors in the statements.

To sum up, the sender, in order to impress the receiver should, at the start, have an idea encoded in the form of a message. At the time of encoding, the sender does a thorough security check to ascertain that all points have been dealt with in a desired order. The message is then transmitted to the receiver with the required voice articulations and pauses so as to heighten the impact. Finally, the response of the receiver should be viewed empathetic ally. Once all these factors have been understood, it proves easy to prevail upon the receiver.

There could, however, be moments when, in spite of efforts being made to make the interaction informative and meaningful, all communication links fall apart and the process ends in a meaningless rumble of words and sounds. This disturbing or distracting factor is what we refer to as *Noise.* This may be on the part of the sender or the receiver; it can be voluntary or involuntary.

NOISE

Noise can be defined as a physical sound or a mental disturbance that disrupts the flow of communication as the sender or the receiver perforce gets distracted by it. According to this definition, noise can be classified into two categories:

1. Physical
2. Psychological.

Physical noise is that sound which emanates from the surroundings and hampers' the listening process, e.g. while speaking on the telephone, disturbances might hinder the smooth transmission of message or just at the time when the sender wishes to transmit an important point, there might be a queer squeaking sound. Physical noise is not all that difficult to manage. It can be done away with at the time of communication by ensuring that all channels are in proper functioning order. For example, often, companies have a soundproof room for discussions.

While care may be taken to eliminate possibilities of physical noise, problems arise at the time when psychological noise plagues either the sender or the receiver. Whenever there is psychological noise, it results in (un)welcome ideas or thoughts crowding the mind, which are of more relevance than the ensuing communication to either of the participants. Listening, as a result, is hampered and responses are not well formulated. Some of the common forms of noise are mental turbulence, preoccupation, ego hang-ups, anxiety, tiredness, pre-conceived ideas and notions. These are mostly involuntary and no cause can be assigned to them.

What is important is awareness about these factors. The sender at a particular moment might be disturbed by psychological noise. If he is aware of the mental turmoil and knows that it would disturb his listening process he should, at the time of communicating, carry a piece of paper and a pen or pencil to jot down points or comments of the receiver. On the other hand, the receiver might also be distracted by psychological noise. Outward manifestations of this disturbance would be in the form of restless tapping on the table, looking in other directions, shifting restlessly, changing positions, etc. These are just some of the means through which the sender can gauge the presence of psychological noise in the mind of the receiver. To make more meaningful and successful communication, the sender should try through certain strategies to draw the attention of the receiver. He can do this by entering into a question answer session or asking for advice. Both these devices would, to a great extent, remove the element of psychological noise.

BARRIERS TO COMMUNICATION

An activity as complex as communication is bound to suffer from setbacks if conditions contrary to the smooth functioning of the process emerge. They are referred to as barriers because they create impediments in the progress of the interaction. Identification of these barriers is extremely important. According to the role observed by the two participants, let us categorise the barriers as:

— Sender-oriented

— Receiver-oriented.

Sender-oriented Barriers

Sender-oriented barriers could be voluntary or involuntary. At any cost, efforts should be made on the part of the sender to identify and remove them. As the sender is the originator of communication, he should be extremely careful not to erect barriers. If his interaction gives rise to or indicates that there are barriers, the communication comes to a grinding halt. Some of the barriers that are sender-oriented are as follows:

Badly expressed message

Not being well versed in the topic under discussion can create problems of this nature. The sender may not be able to structure his ideas accurately and efficiently. What he wishes to say and what he finally imparts may not be the same. The discrepancy emerges as soon as the words are uttered. In fact, one of the important criteria at the time of initialising a piece of communication is that ideas should be concrete and the message should be well structured. The receiver should not feel that the interaction is a waste of time. The moment this feeling crops up, the listener totally switches off and thus ceases the process of effective communication.

Loss in transmission

This is a very minor issue but one that gains in magnitude when it leads to inability in transmitting the actual message. Once again, if the choice of the channel or medium is not right, the impact of the message is lost. This is mostly a physical noise. However, the responsibility lies with the sender, as he should ensure that all channels are free of noise before commencing communication.

Semantic problem

High and big sounding words definitely look and sound impressive. But if the receiver is not able to comprehend the impact of these words, or if they sound 'Greek' or 'Latin' to him, the entire exercise proves futile. This problem could arise in the interpretation of the words or overall meaning of the message. It is also related to the understanding of the intention behind a particular statement. For the receiver, e.g., the sanctity associated with the word "white" might be violated when the receiver uses it in a careless fashion. The idiosyncrasies of the receiver should be well understood by the sender if he does not wish these barriers to crop up at the time of communication. The look on the face of the listener should be sufficient to warn the sender that he has overstepped his limits or he has been misunderstood.

Over/ under communication

The quantum of communication should be just right. Neither should there be excess information nor should it be too scanty. Excess information may confuse the receiver as he has to figure out the exact import of the message, and scanty information would make him grope for the actual intent of the message. The sender should, as far as possible try to get the profile of the receiver so that at the time of communication he knows how much material is needed and how much can be done away with. Suppose he starts with some information that the receiver already possesses, the latter might lose interestas it is merely repetition of what he already knows. So by the time he arrives at the core of the matter, he had already lost the attention of the receiver.

'I'-attitude

Imagine a piece of communication that begins and ends with the pronoun "I". How tedious it is going to be for the listener to sit through the entire piece of interaction. If the sender starts every sentence with "I", it gradually leads to what is referred to as the I-syndrome. He would not be receptive to changes, if suggested by the receiver; as such, changes would go against his personal formulation of certain views.

Prejudices

Starting any piece of communication with a bias or know-it all attitude can prove to be quite detrimental to the growth of communication process. Though it is easier said than done, still, when communication commences, all sorts of prejudices should be done away with, and the mind should be free of bias. This would enable the sender to formulate his message, *Mind, free of* keeping only the receiver and his needs in mind. Thoughts like "Last time he said this..." or "Last time he did this..." or "He belongs to this group..." can totally warp the formulation of the message. This barrier can also be extended to the receiver. If the respondent starts with prejudices in mind, he too would be unable to listen to the intent of the message. His understanding of the message is going to be warped. The messages are going to be understood in relation to the prejudices that a receiver harbours against the sender.

Rules for Overcoming Sender-Oriented Barriers

These barriers are not insurmountable. Care and constant practice on the part of the sender can remove these barriers. Some of the rules for overcoming sender-oriented barriers are as follows:

Plan and clarify ideas

Ideas should be carefully formulated/thought out before beginning any kind of communication. This can be done by following few steps. Primary among them is to test thinking by communicating with peers and colleagues. It is said that two minds are always better than one. Ideas, when discussed aloud with another person, necessarily take on a shape and form. Errors of logic, if any, get sorted out. In this process the concepts of others can also be collated and incorporated to make the communication richer and more fruitful. As these steps require pre-planning and extra time, the sender should be highly motivated. Unless he is sufficiently motivated, he will not spend extra hours in planning the message and clarifying it by facilitating discussions with other members in the organisation.

Create a climate of trust and confidence

In order to win the trust and confidence of the receiver, the sender has to put in extra effort through which he is able to win the trust and confidence of the recipient. This is what we normally refer to as establishing sender credibility. If the receiver is convinced that the sender has his best interests at heart, he would be willing to pay attention to all that is being said and try to grasp the import of the message in the manner in which it is intended.

Time your message carefully

Different occasions and different hours necessitate a change in the encoding of the message. The sender has to be careful of the time and the place he makes his statements. As all communication is situation bound, a statement made at an incorrect moment, or a wrong place can stimulate an undesired response. The most prudent step is to measure the import of the message in relation to the situation and then impart it.

Reinforce words with action

Whatever statements are made should be reinforced by action on the part of the sender. The receiver should not feel that there are two codes at play, one for transmittal and the other for action. If there is harmony between the two, the decoder is mentally at peace, for his grasp is more accurate and thorough.

Communicate efficiently

The sender can only ascertain whether communication has been effective when he confirms with feedback. The receiver on his part is also wary as he knows that he would be requested for feedback. Soliciting and receiving feedback is the simplest and the surest way of removing any barriers that might crop up in the course of communication as a result of either over communication or a semantic problem. Once all barriers to communication have been overcome, communication, it is said has been meaningful and purposeful.

Receiver-Oriented Barriers

Receiver can also have some barriers in the course of the interaction. Although his role in the initial phase is passive, he becomes active when he starts assimilating and absorbing the information. He is equally to blame if the situation goes awry and communication comes to a stop, or there is miscommunication. Some of the barriers emanating from the side of the receiver are as follows:

Poor retention

Retention is extremely important during interaction. If the receiver has poor retention capability, he would probably get lost in the course of the proceedings. There would be no connection between what was said initially and what is being said now. He might counter statements instead of seeking clarifications that might lead to clamping on the part of the sender. If the decoder feels that his retention capacities are not good, a judicious strategy for him would be to jot down points. It does not portray him in a poor light. On the contrary, it shows how conscientious he is to get the message right.

Inattentive listening

The mind has its own way of functioning. It is very

difficult to exercise control over ones mind. Listening is more of an exercise in controlling the mind and exercising it to assimilate messages. The errors in listening arise primarily because the receiver is either not interested in what is being said, or has other things to concentrate on. The art of listening is an exercise in concentration.

Tendency to evaluate

Being judgemental and evaluative are both the starting points for miscommunication. Remember, one mind cannot perform two activities at the same time. If it is evaluating, listening cannot take place. Evaluation should always be a sequel to the listening process. It cannot be done simultaneously with listening. The minute sender opens his mouth, if the listener starts mentally pronouncing judgments concerning his style or content, he has actually missed out on a major part of what has been said. His responses naturally are then going to be incorrect or expose his misunderstanding.

Interests and attitudes

"I am not interested in what you are saying" or "My interest lies in other areas". Starting any piece of communication with this kind of indifference can thwart any attempts at communication. Fixed notions of this kind should be dispensed with. It is not possible to be interested in all that is being said. But to start any communication with this notion is hazardous.

Conflicting information

Dichotomy in the information that the receiver possesses and that which is being transmitted can create confusion and result in miscommunication. Conflict between the existing information and fresh one results in elimination of the latter unless and until the receiver is cautious and verifies with the sender the reliability and validity of the message. The sender should convince the receiver that whatever is now being said is correct and relevant to further proceedings.

Differing status and position

Position in the organisational hierarchy is no criterion to determine the strength of ideas and issues. Rejecting the proposal of a subordinate or harbouring a misconception that a junior cannot come up with a "eureka" concept is not right. In fact, many companies have started encouraging youngsters to come up with ideas/ solutions to a particular problem. These ideas are then discussed among the senior managers and their validity is ascertained keeping the workings and the constraints of the company in mind. The basic purpose of this upward traversing of ideas is that fresh and innovative minds can come up with unique solutions. If an individual has been working in a particular company for some years, it is natural that his mind gets conditioned in a particular manner. Challenging newcomers to innovate, as a part of company policy takes care of ego problems that may arise if this is not a accepted norm.

Resistance to change

Fixed ideas, coupled with an unwillingness to change or discuss, hampers listening and results in miscommunication. Novae concepts that require discussion before they can really materialise, if rebuked, fall flat. The onus lies directly on the receiver who is unreceptive and unwilling to change. People with dogmatic opinions and views prove to be very poor communicators and erect maximum number of barriers.

Refutations and arguments

Refutations and arguments are negative in nature. Trying to communicate with the sender on the premise that refutations and arguments can yield fruitful results would prove to be futile. Communication is a process in which the sender and the *healthy receiver* are at the same level. The minute refutations or *discussions* arguments begin, there is a shift in balance between the two participants, after which the receiver moves to a conceived higher position and the sender remains at the same level. In case there are some contradictions that need to be resolved, discussion is the right way to approach. Listening to the views of the other, trying to understand or at least showing that there has been understanding, appreciating and, finally, positing own views should be the sequence to be followed. The strategy adopted should not make the sender feel small or slighted.

3

QUESTIONING SKILLS

Effective questioning is a real compliment to your skills. It shows that you have the ability to understand the caller's real needs. It shows that you are looking for meaning that's deeper than the spoken message. Effective questioning is a powerful, learned skill. It says to the caller, "I'm interested in determining your needs."

Questioning can be put into two divisions: Open-Ended Questions and Closed-Ended Questions.

Open-ended questions: Open-ended questions are questions without a fixed limit. They encourage continued conversation, and help you get more information. Plus, they often provide opportunities to gain insight into the other person's feelings. Open-ended questions draw out more information. If you want the caller to open up, use open-ended questions that start with who, what, where, why, when, and how. A few examples are:

- "What are some of the things you look for in a hotel?"
- "How do you feel government could be more responsive to your needs?"
- "What are your concerns about this new programme?"

Closed-ended questions: Closed-ended questions have a fixed limit. They're often answered with a yes or no, or with a simple statement of fact. Closed-ended questions are used to direct the conversation. They usually get specific information or confirm facts. Here are some examples.

- "Do you have health insurance?"
- "Do you want the new brochure?"
- "Would you be interested in that?"

We use the open-ended questions to get more information and the closed-ended questions to focus in on one area. Additionally, there are several other type of questioning techniques. A few are:

Probing questions: Sometimes you ask an open-ended question to get more information and you only get part of what you need. Now it's time for a probing question. A probing question is another open-ended question, but it's a follow-up. It's narrower. It asks about one area. Here's an example:

"What topic areas are you interested in?" This question would be better than reading off 50 topics to the caller. It's a probing question. A few other examples are:

- "Are you able to tell me more about the form you received?"
- "What did you like best about Buddhists?"

Probing questions are valuable in getting to the heart of the matter.

The echo question: Here's a good technique for getting more information. You can use this like a probing question. The idea is to use the last part of a phrase the caller said. Slightly raise the tone of your voice at the end of the phrase to convert it to a question. Then pause and use silence - like this:

— "...The bill you received?"

An echo question repeats part of the phrase that the caller used, using voice inflection to convert it to a question. Some people call it mirroring or reflecting. Others call it parroting. We call it echoing. Whatever you call it, it's a valuable technique to use.

Leading questions: Many things can be good or bad. Take fire for example. Fire warms our home, cooks our food, and does many other useful things. Uncontrolled, it can burn down our houses.

The reason we use that example is because leading questions can also be good or bad. Leading questions, if used improperly, can be manipulative because you're leading the person to give the answer you want. When they are used properly, you're helping that person.

Leading questions often end with suggestive nudges toward the desired answer. Some ending phrases would be, "Don't you?", "Shouldn't you?", "Won't you?", "Haven't you?", and "Right?"

So where are leading questions useful? Well, they're useful in helping someone who's undecided make the right decision, a decision that will benefit them. You use a leading question ethically when you help someone do the right thing. Some folks call this technique the "tie down" technique because you're actually trying to tie down the caller's needs.

The bottom line is to practice using a variety of questioning techniques. It will help you help your callers more effectively. After all, you want to provide the very best customer service, don't you?

CHUNKING QUESTIONS

Chunking is a simple technique to use during questioning to vary the level of detail of information you get.

Chunking Down

Sometimes the person you are talking with is speaking at a very high level, covering general ideas and themes. Leaders often like to think this way, with grand plans and visions.

Sometimes you deliberately started this way, getting a big picture before you dive into detail.

Chunking down is getting more detail by probing for more information about the high-level information you already have. The goal is to find out more, fill in the empty gaps in your picture, test the reality of the situation, and so on.

The more you ask chunking questions, the more you will find further detail. Keep going and you'll soon end up in the weeds. In fact if you go too deep, you can get lost. A tip: try to stay within three chunking levels for most of the time, digging deeper only on topics of particular interest where you want to bottom out the subject. Chunk down by asking questions such as:

- How did you that?
- Why did that happen?
- What happened about...?
- What, specifically,...
- Tell me more about...
- What is the root cause of all this?

Chunking Up

Sometimes the person you are talking with is already down in the details. Some people are happiest when they have their teeth sunk into the grit of a tangible problem. Yet it can also help them if they come up for air some time and see the big picture - and maybe find they were digging in the wrong place...

To chunk up, you are doing the opposite of chunking down - looking for a more generalised understanding. This includes looking for overall purpose, meaning, linkages, etc.

Chunk up by asking questions such as:

— What does this mean?

— Let's look at the bigger picture...

— How does that relate to...?

— What are we trying to achieve here?

— Who is this for? What do they really want?

CLEAR QUESTIONS

Sometimes you want to use questions that not clear for specific reasons, but most of the time, when you are seeking honest answers, you will want to ask questions that allow the other person to answer exactly how they feel. Even when your intent is for clear answers, it is easy to ask what you think is a nice and easy question and then find that they are confused and perhaps even answer a completely different question. Here are a few things to remember.

Non-leading Questions

Leading questions have their place, but not if you want to get unbiased answers. Think carefully about how the other person may interpret the question.

Non-emotional Questions

Questions that display emotion may lead the other person to seek to calm you down. They may also lead to them getting empathetically wound up. The stronger the emotion, the greater the effect. Questions that lead them into emotional states will also have an impact on their responses. If not for this question then possibly for subsequent ones. One way of avoiding emotion is to talk in the third person, taking yourself and especially them out of the picture. Thus, rather than say:

> "Do other drivers make you feel angry?"

You might say instead:

> "Have you seen people being annoyed by other drivers?"

Avoid Jargon

Jargon is useful for people who specialise in the same subject as it allows them to talk in 'shorthand'. It is sometimes useful to use it with other people to signal your expertise. Most of the time, however, it just annoys other people.

Avoid Complex Language

Academics and writers love to play with big words. It is their medium and utilisation of complex verbiage creates essential stimulatory excitation for them. It also often falls into a form of jargon. Sadly or otherwise, most of us have a very limited vocabulary. Of the 25000 or more words in the English language, only about 2000 (or less!) are used in many everyday conversations.

FUNNEL QUESTIONING

Funnel questioning seeks further information either that goes into more specific detail or becomes more general.

Increasing Detail

You can use questions to find out increasing detail about some particular topic of interest. This narrows the funnel, giving you more information about a smaller area.

Increasing detail is similar to deductive reasoning, where thinking goes from general to more specific.

Say 'Tell me more about'

Asking 'tell me more' is a very open and general question that also focuses the other person on a particular area, giving you more information about this. As an open question it allows the other person more leeway in what they say and gets you more detail. This causes a slower convergence (but this may not be a bad thing).

> Person: I was leaving the building and had to wait until a red truck moved before I could get to my car.
>
> You: Tell me more about the red truck.
>
> Person: It was a Malters truck, I think, with a long yellow stripe down the side.
>
> You: What do you remember about the yellow stripe.

Use Precision Words

Using words like 'specifically', 'actually' or 'particularly' gives the person subtle direction to give you more detail in a particular direction. Use these alongside Kipling questions such as 'What', 'How' and 'When'.

> You said that the person told you they were leaving. What, specifically, did they say?
>
> When exactly did you go home?
>
> Who in particular seemed interested in the presentation?

Decreasing Detail

The reverse of narrowing the funnel is to broaden the funnel, asking questions that give you less specific information and more information about more general topics.

Decreasing detail is similar to inductive reasoning, where thinking goes from specific to more general.

Use broadening questions

Use questions that give you less detail about a small area and more information about related topics. Thus ask 'Who else', 'What else', etc.

> What other things are you planning on doing?
>
> Who else will be there?

Use vague questions

You can also use vague questions. When the real purpose of the question is not clear, the other person has more leeway to answer the question in any associated way.

> So what do you think?
>
> What else?

GROUP QUESTIONING

When you are asking questions of a group, whether it is a studio audience, a focus group a class of students or something else, there are a number of traps you can fall into.

Who are You Asking?

When you ask within a group, you can ask in a number of directions - and you should be clear so people in the group know how to answer. A general question asked to thin air may get no answer as people either think it is rhetorical or are not sure if you asking them.

Ask an individual

When asking an individual, use their name, point to them, say 'the person in the red hat' or otherwise ensure that they know you are asking them in particular.

Give them a moment or two to realise that they are being asked a question. A way of doing this is to first indicate that you are asking them a question, or even ask if you can ask. Thus

> 'Rohit, can I ask you a question about this?'

Ask a selection

To ask a subset from the group, first qualify them, and also let them know how they should make themselves visible. For example:

> 'Who here has got a Maruti car? Please put your hands up.'

Asking everyone

Even if you are asking the group as a whole, again give them a prompt to let them know that they should wake up and start thinking. You can do this by asking for a volunteer:

> 'Who can tell me what this means?'

Keeping them with you

It is easy in a group to go to sleep or otherwise zone out. Keep them with you by being interesting and ensuring they are engaged at all times.

Scanning

Keep looking around to see whether people are showing interest, confusion, agitation, etc. And then respond accordingly, of course. Ask those who look confused or agitated what the problem is, or ask them something to engage them (but beware of tirades, of course).

Pointing

Point yourself at everybody from time to time. This does not need a finger - all you need is to point your body. Range back and forth looking down lines and diagonals of people (all in the line will think you are looking at them). Look into eyes - not just scanning but pausing on people but not staring, of course.

Rehearsing

Help them think by talking what they perhaps should be thinking. This may mean musing about meaning, summarising understanding so far, making tentative conclusions. Then look out to see if they are with you, of course.

Repeating

When you have an answer from someone, it is often good to repeat it back to the group as many will not have heard it clearly. A way of doing this in combination with testing your understanding of the answer is to repeat it back to the person who answered in the form of a question. Thus:

> 'Thanks, Jim, so you think we should all learn to fly, is that right?'

Engaging

Engage individual in short conversations, but beware of being dragged into something longer. Also beware of falling into a comfort zone of talking only with those who you like. Engage the whole group allowing multiple inputs with such as:

> 'Who else has an opinion on this?'

Steering

A key element of working with a group is steering them in the direction you want them to go.

Reward and punishment

Asking individuals focuses attention of everyone else on that individual, and how you respond to them will signal to others what to do next. If you criticise them, then few others will volunteer. If you praise or otherwise reward them, then they and others will be more motivated to respond.

Attention

The attention you pay to what is said is a signal to

If you pick up and praise them on a particular point, then the conversation will turn in that direction.

> 'That's a great point about long-term cost, Sue. Who else can add something about this?'

Concluding

To steer a group towards the end of a session, summarise the whole session and perhaps allow a few more inputs to let people get what is on their mind at the moment whilst also blocking any new topics.

> 'We have five minutes left. Does anyone have any last comments to make?'

Notice the word 'last', which signals that the conclusion is rapidly approaching. The time comment is also a very clear signal.

Always end, by the way, with thanks. It may also help to tell them what will happen next (if this is relevant to them).

INTERROGATION QUESTIONS

Here are a set of question types that can be used through an interrogation of any kind.

Opening Questions

Start off the interrogation with easy closed questions that the other person can answer. Stay off the main topic at least until they are talking freely.

The purpose of these questions is to break the ice whilst creating a degree or rapport.

> Are you warm? Would you like a cigarette? Have they treated you well?

Ensure you establish yourself as the person who asks questions. If they ask questions back and especially if it seems as if they are trying to take control, either ignore them or give short or non-committal answers, whilst retaining a friendly or neutral manner. If you do allow questioning, do so with a clear purpose, for example to deliberately let them think they are not in any trouble such that you can provide a shock to them at a designed point.

Free Narrative Questions

Name a subject, for example a time and place, and then ask the other person to tell you what they know about this. Then stay silent and do not interrupt or probe during the answer. Let them tell you about the situation in their own words.

> I hear you were on the platform when the person near you fell onto the rails. Could you please describe what happened?

Show a steady mild interest and do not become excited when they get into relevant detail.

Their answer will first tell you the degree to which the person is initially ready to collaborate. You can also listen for gaps and contradictions to probe at a later time, as well as indicators of preferences, needs and other motivators.

Direct Questions

Follow up the free narrative with direct questions about specific items. Keep the questions free from value-laden words that might imply guilt. Ask one simple question at a time to which a clear answer can be given.

> When you fought with the other person, did he hit you? [direct question]
>
> When you attacked the other person, did he try to defend himself? [value-laden question]

The answers to these questions will give you specific detail, filling in the holes of their initial story and exposing areas where they may be unwilling to talk. However, having told you the story beforehand, they are now much more willing to support their original narrative.

Cross-questioning

Ask multiple questions at different times about the same thing to see whether their answers support or contradict one another. You can appear unintelligent or confused as necessary to cloak your repetition.

> When you went into the back of the shop, where was Romy standing?
>
> ...
>
> What did Romy do as you were going back there?
>
> ...
>
> Sorry, I don't quite understand — what was Romy doing all this while?

If answers are contradictory, carefully probe further, asking more diagonal questions that allow them to expose themselves without necessarily realising what is happening.

Review Questions

Review questions are used to summarise and test your understanding of what you have heard so far. State what you understand and ask for agreement or otherwise.

> So Romy came out after Vinod, is that correct?

Review points can also be used to 'squeeze the lemon' for any more information.

> Is there anything else that you can tell me about this?
>
> What else were you expecting me to ask?

Review points can be used at natural break points, such as in changes of scene. They are also useful at the end, to summarise.

Reviews can also be used in a deceptive way, asking for agreement of things that you know are wrong. This tests the person's honesty and may also be used to trick them into thinking that you have missed key points. When doing this, watch their body language and signs of duper's delight.

KIPLING QUESTIONS

Rudyard Kipling wrote a short poem outlining a powerful set of questions:

> I keep six honest serving men
>
> (They taught me all I knew);
>
> Their names are What and Why and When
>
> And How and Where and Who.

Whenever in doubt as to what to ask, just dip into these questions.

What

'What?' often asks for noun responses, seeking things that are or will be. They may also seek verbs when they seek actions. 'What' questions include:

> What are you doing?
>
> What shall we do next?
>
> What happened?
>
> What is stopping you from succeeding?
>
> What is the most important thing to do now?

Three 'Whats' that may be asked in sequence to solve problems are:

What are you trying to achieve?

What is the real problem?

What is the solution?

Why

Asking 'why' seeks cause-and-effect. If you know the reason why people have done something, then you gain a deeper understanding of them. If you know how the world works, then you may be able to affect how it changes in the future.

Asking 'why' seeks logical connections and shows you to be rational in your thinking. It can also be a good way of creating a pause or distraction in a conversation, as many people make assertive statements but without knowing the real 'why' behind those assertions.

A reversal of 'Why' is to ask 'Why not', which is a wonderful creative problem for stimulating people to think 'outside the box'. Why questions include:

Why did you do that?

Why did that happen?

Why is it important for us to try it again?

Why not give it a try?

When

'When' seeks location in time and can imply two different types of time. 'When', first of all, can ask for a specific single time, for example when a person will arrive at a given place or when an action will be completed. 'When' may also seek a duration, a period of time, such as when a person will take a holiday.

When will you be finished?

When will you give me the money?

When are you taking your holiday? (next Summer)

How

'How' seeks verbs of process. They thus are good for probing into deeper detail of what has happened or what will happen.

How did you achieve that?

How shall we get there?

How will you know she likes you?

'How' may also be used with other words to probe into time and quantity.

How often will you see me?

How much do you owe him?

Where

'Where' seeks to locate an action or event in three-dimensional space. This can be simple space, such as on, above, under, below. It can be regional space, such as next door or in the other building. It can be geographic space, such as New Delhi, London or Tokyo.

If something is going to be delivered or done, then asking 'Where' is a very good companion to asking 'When' to clarify exactly what delivery will take place.

Where will you put it?

Where will they be delivered?

Who

The question 'Who' brings people into the frame, connecting them with actions and things. The 'Who' of many situations includes 'stakeholders', who are all the people who have an interest in the action. Key people to identify are those who will pay for and receive the benefits of the action. Of course, you also may want to know who is going to do the work and whose neck is on the line — that is who is ultimately responsible.

> Who is this work for?
>
> Who will benefit most from what you propose?
>
> Who else would be interested?

Assumptive Questions

Kipling questions provide a simple method of using assumptive questions that act as if something is true, then hide it in a question:

> How much do you care? (assumption: you care)
>
> How will you persuade her? (assumption: you will seek to persuade her)
>
> Where will you buy it? (assumption: you will buy it)
>
> When will you make the change? (assumption: you will make the change)

Solving Problems

A simple framework for solving problems may be defined by combining What, Why and How, as follows:

1. What is the problem?
2. Why is it happening?
3. How can you fix it?
4. -Fix it! -
5. Why did it work or not work?
6. What next?

LEADING QUESTIONS

One way of influencing a person is to ask them questions that are deliberately designed to make them think in a certain way. Leading questions either include the answer, point the listener in the right direction or include some form or carrot or stick to send them to the 'right' answer.

Note that not only the words can lead the question, you can also lead people by your body Language and voice tone effects such as emphasis.

Leading questions are often directional in that, whilst they do not indicate an answer, they close off undesirable alternatives and guide the person in a desired direction.

Assumptive Questions

Leading questions can use Assumption principle, for example by moving the subject of the sentence:

> "How much will prices go up next year?"

This assumes that prices will go up next year - the subject of the question is about how much prices will go up. In fact it is very difficult to avoid assumptions. Even if you said:

> "Do you think prices will go up next year?"

...you are still forcing the other person to think first and possibly exclusively about prices going up (If they answer 'no' then this may mean they will be stable - a thought about them going down may not have been made).

Linked Statements

You can lead questions using the Association principle by things you said previously and are still in the mind of the person being questioned. For example:

> "I really hate this government!!...What are your thoughts about the XX party?"

You can also put something within the question.

> "What do you think about John Richards? Many people are opposed to him, by the way."

Note the social coercion in this statement.

You could also add desirable carrots in the statement:

> "Would you prefer to live in Alba or in Barta, where the crime rate is very low."

Note that the crime rate in Alba is not mentioned, but the link of low crime with Barta will still make it more desirable.

Implication Questions

Asking questions that gets the other person to think of consequences or implications of current or past events links the past with the future in an inescapable chain of cause-and-effect.

> "If you go to the party tonight, what will happen in your examination tomorrow?"

> "If you vote for that party, then what do you think will happen to taxes? What happened last time they were in power?"

Ask for Agreement

A very direct leading question is where they are closed questions that clearly ask for agreement, making it easier for the other person to say 'yes' than 'no'.

> "Do you agree that we need to save the whales?"

> "Is it true that you are happier now?"

Tag Questions

Tag questions are short questions that are tagged onto the end of statements. They effectively make a command look like a question. They are short phrases and often include a negative element such as 'Isn't it?' or 'Don't you?' or 'Aren't you?'

Thus you might say:

> "That's a good thing to do, isn't it?"

Or:

> "You'll come to dinner tonight, won't you?"

Tag questions can used to add a confusion element:

> "I wonder if you're feeling better now, aren't you?"

Coercive Questions

Questions that force specific answers can include implicit or explicit coercion. Thus:

> "You are coming tonight, aren't you? If you aren't then there will be trouble."
>
> "How can you say you won't come?"
>
> "You do love me, don't you?"

OPEN AND CLOSED QUESTIONS

These are two types of questions you can use that are very different in character and usage.

Closed Questions

A closed question can be answered with either a single word or a short phrase. Thus 'How old are you?' and 'Where do you live?' are closed questions. Closed questions have the following characteristics:

- They give you facts.
- They are easy to answer.
- They are quick to answer.
- They keep control of the conversation with the questioner.

Note how you can turn any opinion into a closed question that forces a yes or no by adding tag questions, such as "isn't it?", "don't you?" or "can't they?" to any statement.

The first word of a question sets up the dynamic of the closed question, signaling the easy answer ahead. Note how these are words like: do, would, are, will, if.

Open Questions

An open question is likely to receive a long answer. Although any question can receive a long answer, open questions deliberately seek longer answers, and are the opposite of closed questions.

Open questions have the following characteristics:

- They ask the respondent to think and reflect.
- They will give you opinions and feelings.
- They hand control of the conversation to the respondent.

Open questions begin with such as: what, why, how, describe.

Using open questions can be scary, as they seem to hand the baton of control over to the other person. However, well-placed questions do leave you in control as you steer their interest and engage them where you want them.

When opening conversations, a good balance is around three closed questions to one open question. The closed questions start the conversation and summarise progress, whilst the open question gets the other person thinking and continuing to give you useful information about them.

A neat trick is to get them to ask you open questions. This then gives you the floor to talk about what you want. The way to achieve this is to intrigue them with an incomplete story or benefit.

POSITIVE QUESTIONS

You can get what you want from others by deliberately using leading questions that encourage people to agree with you.

Underlying Principles

Positive questioning is based on two principles.

Yes is better than no

Disagreement is a generally uncomfortable experience. It may be considered impolite. When you disagree, you are risking argument, and to argue is to risk failure.

In comparison with the risk and discomfort of disagreement, agreement is generally preferable. When you phrase questions, you should thus generally make a positive response lead to that which you seek.

Speaking creates

When you say something, then in order to understand what you are saying, the other person has to fully contemplate what you say. Thus if you say 'do not stand up', then they have to think about standing up in order to decide whether or not to comply, whereas if you said 'stay sitting down' then all they need to do is think about is sitting down.

In asking positive questions, you should thus only say that which you want the other person to contemplate and avoid that which you do not want them to contemplate.

Questions that Lead

By using the above questions, the other person can be led into action or otherwise.

Creating positive action

To get somebody to do something positive, ask them by naming the action, and phrased such that saying 'yes' leads to agreement and compliance.

Will you do this work?

I was wondering if you would like to go out with me?

Can you help me take this upstairs?

Will you take a lower sum?

Dissuading action

To get somebody to consider not doing something, whilst appearing to be encouraging them to do

Do you mind very much doing this work?

I know you might not want to go out with me, but will you?

Are you just going to sit there watching the football?

Will you move from the price that you have fixed?

Preventing action

To get someone not do do something, use positive framing of the negative task.

Would you prefer to do something else?

Who else do you want to go out with?

Do you want to watch the football?

Do you want me to agree to your price?

PROBING QUESTIONS

There are a number of types probes you can use, depending on what they are saying and what you want to discover.

Clarification

When they are vague or have not given enough information, seek to further understand them by asking for clarification.

What exactly did you mean by 'XXX'?

What, specifically, will you do next week?

Could you tell me more about YY?

Purpose

Sometimes they say things where the purpose of why they said it is not clear. Ask them to justify their statement or dig for underlying causes.

Why did you say that?

What were you thinking about when you said XX?

Relevance

If they seem to be going off-topic, you can check whether what they are saying is relevant to the main purpose of inquiry.

Is that relevant to the main question?

How is what you are saying related to what I asked?

Completeness and Accuracy

You can check that they are giving you a full and accurate account by probing for more detail and checking against other information you have. Sometimes people make genuine errors, which you may want to check.

Is that all? Is there anything you have missed out?

How do you know that is true?

How does that compare with what you said before?

Repetition

One of the most effective ways of getting more detail is simply by asking the same question again. You can use the same words or you can rephrase the question (perhaps they did not fully understand it first time).

Where did you go?

...

What places did you visit?

You can also repeat what they have said ('echo question'), perhaps with emphasis on the area where you want more detail.

He asked you to marry him??

Examples

When they talk about something vaguely, you may ask for specific examples. This is particularly useful in interviews, where what you want to test both their truthfulness and the depth behind what they are claiming.

Sorry, I don't understand. Could you help by giving an example?

Could you give me an example of when you did XXX?

Tell me about a time when you ___.

Extension

When they have not given you enough information about something, ask them to tell you more.

Could you tell me more about that, please?

And what happened after that?

Then...

Evaluation

To discover both how judgmental they are and how they evaluate, use evaluative question:

How good would you say it is?

How do you know it is worthless?

What are the pros and cons of this situation?

Emotional

Particularly if they are talking in the third person or otherwise unemotionally and you want to find out how they feel, you can ask something like:

And how did you feel about that?

When you do this, do be careful: you may have just asked a cathartic question that results in them exploding with previously-suppressed emotion.

QUESTIONING TRAPS

When questioning another person, there are many traps for the unwary questioner that can lead you into deep water. Instead of digging into their knowledge, you end up digging a hole for yourself.

Here are a few of the things you may want to avoid.

Bias

It is very easy when questioning to let your own values, preferences and biases to leak into what you are asking. This can have a number of unhelpful effects, including most of those below. If in doubt and if you can, get someone else to review your questions before you ask them of your target.

> What do you think about the problems that disabled people are causing?

Leading Questions

Leading questions are those that nudge, push or shove the other person towards a particular answer and away from other answers. They are a very common form of bias. Closed questions can be particularly susceptible to this trap.

> Do you think that the government is having problems?
>
> Would you say that this product is well-presented?

Note how the answer is embedded into these question (e.g. 'the government is having problems'). Note also how they questions are fairly general and easy to say 'yes' to.

> Do you think that the government is the worst that has ever been?

Would you say that this product will make every surface in your home perfectly clean?

Now it is easy to fall the other way, as you are leading them into saying 'no'. By asking an absolute question, you give them lots of space in which 'no' is a correct answer. Saying 'yes' commits them to an extreme position - and few people like to be put into a corner.

Interrogation

Interested questioning can easily turn into the Spanish Inquisition, and unless you have got the other person tied to the chair, they can easily get up and leave, at least psychologically. They might also fight back.

Are you ready for this? Why not? What have you been doing all week?

Listen to both yourself and their answers. If you are talking quickly or their answers are getting shorter, back off for a while or otherwise slow down the proceedings.

Negativity

Sometimes, negativity in questions turns the other person off. Even accidental use of negative words can lead them to feel negative and consequently unwilling to answer further questions.

What problems have you had recently?

For example, if the word 'problem' could tip the other person into thinking negatively, you might use words such as: difficulty, challenge, complaint, obstacle, hassle, etc. or otherwise phrase the question to help the person answer honestly.

What keeps you awake at night?

Digression

There are many places where you can go in conversation that lead off the area of your main interest. It may be of interest to you and it may be of interest to the other person, but other than a little happiness, it can lose you time, information and commitment.

Privacy

Another quagmire where you can sink without trace is if you get into an area which the other person feels is private and where you are not really welcome.

Look for signs of discomfort and decide whether you really need to stay in this difficult territory.

RESPONDING TO QUESTIONS

Questioning can be a method of control in a conversation, and when many are asked questions, they respond without thinking of the opportunity that gives them to steer the conversation in the direction they want. Here are a few ways.

Pause for Thought

Rather than try to answer the question straight away, pause for a moment.

Don't be hurried. Hurrying is a technique used to try and stop you thinking. If the other person is talking fast, it may be because they are a visual thinker and it may be because they are trying to hurry you up.

Pausing for thought can help your credibility too. It seems as if you are taking the other person seriously as you carefully consider their question. This is considered to be normal and polite in some countries (e.g. Japan).

Answer with a Surprise

Rather than give the answer they expect, change tack with something outside of the normal range of answers.

Be candid

Tell the truth when it might not be expected. Break with custom. When you are asked 'How are you', tell them. If your answer might be disagreed with, be disarmingly honest. Say things that are supposedly damaging to your own credibility.

Shower them with detail

Give them more information than they expected. If you shower them with lots of detail, it will cause cognitive overload. Talking a lot also has a filibustering effect, where you prevent them from saying anything else and use up the time available for the conversation.

Answer with a Question

Answering a question with a question is a great way of avoiding answering, at least for the moment. It gives you time to think. Done well, it will result in them trying to answer your question and maybe forgetting the question they were asking in the first place (it is at the very least a good test of how interested and determined they are).

Ask for more detail

Dig further into the topic. Ask them to explain more. Be Socratic in seeking to get them to answer the question, leading them to the answer with your questions.

Question the question

Challenge the question being asked. Ask whether it is the right question to ask. Suggest there are other questions first.

Question the questioner

Challenge the right of the person to ask the question. Question their legitimacy as a person to ask questions ('Who gave you the right to ask that?').

Ask a completely different question

You can also ask a completely different question. This will usually throw the other person off their tracks, particularly if you persist with further questions on the same track.

Ignore the Question

A method used by many politicians is simply to ignore the question and say what you have to say anyway. A typical sharp steer is 'That's a very good question, but what I really want to say is...'.

Ignoring people and their questions is a breech of social rules and hence is a power move. If you can get away with ignoring the question or the questioner, you will have acquired power that lets you repeat this action.

RHETORICAL QUESTIONS

Rhetorical questions are not really questions, but statements given in question format.

Public speakers often use rhetorical questions in the middle of speeches. Of course, the audience cannot all answer, but the intent is to engage them in thinking and consider what answer they would give if they could.

Hedging

We use rhetorical questions sometimes when we want to make a statement but are not confident enough to assert a point. The question format thus allows others to disagree, but is not necessarily seeking agreement of

Isn't that wonderful? Is it a shade of blue?

Self-talk

Sometimes when you ask questions, you are really asking them of yourself rather than the other person. This is particularly noticeable when you give the answer soon after asking the question.

> What is that? A bird, I'd say. What type? Maybe an eagle? I think so. What a lovely flight path.

Multiple Questions

When you ask multiple questions at once, you seldom expect them all to be answered, and perhaps none of them.

They become particularly rhetorical when you do not give time for the other person to answer.

> Where have you been? What time do you think this is? Do you think you can come home late like this and nobody notice?

Terminating Statement

Another way that stopping the other person from answering is to put a statement of some sort immediately after the question.

There is thus no space for the person to answer the question and are directed more by the final statement than the question.

> Can you see? Look there!

SELLING WITH QUESTIONS

When selling, you do not need to be always giving your sales pitch. With a smart use of questions, you can get your customer to sell to themselves. Here are a few ways you can use questions. Then go to the questioning techniques page to find further ideas.

Learning Questions

First of all, questions give you useful information. Information is power, of course, and can offer you all kinds of ways to sell. Frame questions to find out more about how and where the customer will be using the product. Find out the problems they have which your products will solve.

> Where will you be wearing this?
>
> How often do you clean the floors?

Bonding Questions

Questions can also help to create bonding between you and your customer. Show an interest in them by asking them questions to demonstrate that you care, personally, about them. We buy things from people we like. So encourage them to like you.

> What did you do at the weekend? ... I saw the game, too! Wasn't it great?
>
> You look sad — what's the matter?

Teaching Questions

Questions can also be used to teach them about the product, eliciting opinions or perhaps asking rhetorical questions that require no real answer. Teaching questions get the person to think and draw conclusions for themselves.

> Do you know how long this filter will last?
>
> Can you imagine taking this home today?

Closing Questions

You can also ask questions to move a customer towards closing. Closing questions encourage the person to decide that they want to buy what you are selling.

> How would this look like at home?
>
> When would you like to place the order?

SOCRATIC QUESTIONS

Socrates was one of the greatest educators who taught by asking questions and thus drawing out answers from his pupils. Sadly, he martyred himself by drinking hemlock rather than compromise his principles. Bold, but not a good survival strategy. But then he lived very frugally and was known for his eccentricity. His pupils, by the way, include Plato and Aristotle. Plato wrote up much what we know of him.

Here are the six types of questions that Socrates asked his pupils. Probably often to their initial annoyance but more often to their ultimate delight. He was a man of remarkable integrity and his story makes for marvellous reading.

The overall purpose, by the way, is to challenge accuracy and completeness of thinking in a way that acts to move people towards their ultimate goal. Don't waste time by doing it for your own gratification. Get your kicks vicariously, from the movement you create.

Conceptual Clarification Questions

Get them to think more about what exactly they are asking or thinking about. Prove the concepts behind their argument. Basic 'tell me more' questions that get them to go deeper.

- Why are you saying that?
- What exactly does this mean?
- How does this relate to what we have been talking about?
- What is the nature of ...?
- What do we already know about this?
- Can you give me an example?
- Are you saying ... or ... ?

— Can you rephrase that, please?

Probing Rationale, Reasons and Evidence

When they give a rationale for their arguments, dig into that reasoning rather than assuming it is a given. People often use un-thought-through or weakly understood supports for their arguments.

— Why is that happening?

— How do you know this?

— Show me ... ?

— Can you give me an example of that?

— What do you think causes ... ?

— What is the nature of this?

— Are these reasons good enough?

— Would it stand up in court?

— How might it be refuted?

— How can I be sure of what you are saying?

— Why is ... happening?

— Why?

— What evidence is there to support what you are saying?

— On what authority are you basing your argument?

Questioning Viewpoints and Perspectives

Most arguments are given from a particular position. So attack the position. Show that there are other, equally valid, viewpoints.

— Another way of looking at this is ..., does this seem reasonable?

— What alternative ways of looking at this are there?

— Why it is ... necessary?

— Who benefits from this?
— What is the difference between... and...?
— Why is it better than ...?
— What are the strengths and weaknesses of...?
— How are ... and ... similar?
— What would ... say about it?
— What if you compared ... and ... ?
— How could you look another way at this?

Questions about the Question

And you can also get reflexive about the whole thing, turning the question in on itself. Use their attack against themselves. Bounce the ball back into their court, etc.

— What was the point of asking that question?
— Why do you think I asked this question?
— What does that mean?

TAG QUESTIONS

Tag questions are small questions added to the end of a statement, for example:

That is a dog, isn't it?

Structure of Tags

Here are a range of tag questions:

— ..., won't you?
— ..., can't you?
— ..., shouldn't you?
— ..., don't they?
— ..., isn't it?
— ..., won't it?

Note the structural elements:

- — The first element contains a verb, often 'to be' or 'to do', and is often a repetition of the verb used in the statement.
- — The verb is negated, in the abbreviated form.
- — The second element is a pronoun.

Using Tag Questions

Use tag questions to emphasize and encourage the other person to agree. They turn a bold assertion into a question that is difficult to disagree with.

Gaining agreement

Make an assertion and add a tag question:

> They will finish, won't they?
>
> I am the best person for the job, aren't I?
>
> This is the best way to do it, isn't it?

Gaining compliance

Start with what you want the other person to do, and then end with a tag such as 'won't you' or 'can't you'.

> You will come to the dance, won't you?
>
> You can do this today, can't you?

4

LISTENING SKILLS

Listening is the ability to understand and respond effectively to Oral communication. Thus, we can state at the outset that hearing is not listening. Listening requires more than hearing; it requires understanding of the communication received.

Poor listening habits can keep an organisation from functioning properly. Industrial firms have recognised the importance of the listening skill to managers for some time. In his role as a executive counsellor at Johnson and Johnson, Dr. Earl Planty said: "By far the most effective method by which executives can tap ideas of subordinates is sympathetic listening in the many day-to-day informal contacts within and outside the work place. There is no system that will do the job in an easier manner. Nothing can equal an executive's willingness to listen."

The benefits of applied listening skills are impressive. Good listeners make a company a more effective organisation. They have better rapport with others, they get more out of meetings and are more effective in conferences, and they are better at understanding the needs of others.

COMMON FAULTS OF LISTENING

Research studies shows that our listening efficiency is no better than 25 to 30 per cent. That means the considerable information is lost in the listening process. Why? Some reasons are as follows:

1. *Prejudice against the speaker*—At times we have conflict in our mind as to the speaker. Whatever he speaks seems to be coloured and we practically don't listen what he says.
2. *Rehearsing*—Your whole attention is on designing and preparing your next comment. You look interested, but your mind is going a mile a minute because you are thinking about what to say next. Some people rehearse whole chains of responses: I'll say, then he'll say, and so on.
3. *Judging negatively*—Labelling people can be extremely limiting. If you prejudge somebody as incompetent or uninformed, you don't pay much attention to what that person says. A basic rule of listening is that judgments should only be made after you have heard and evaluated the content of the message.
4. *Identifying*—When using this block, you take everything people tell you and refer it back to your own experience. They want to tell you about a toothache, but that reminds you of your oral surgery for receding gums. You launch into your story before they can finish theirs.
5. *Advising*—You are the great problem solver. You don't have to hear more than a few sentences before you begin searching for the right advice. However, while you are coming up with suggestions and convincing someone to just try it, you may miss what is most important.

6. *Sparring*—This block has you arguing and debating with people who never feel heard because you are so quick to disagree. In fact, your main focus is on finding things to disagree with.
7. *Being Right*—Being right means you will go to great lengths to -avoid being wrong. You can't listen to criticism, you can't be corrected, and you can't take suggestions to change.
8. *Derailing*—This listening block involves suddenly changing the subject. You derail the train of conversation when you get uncomfortable or bored with a topic. Another way of derailing is by joking.
9. *Placating*—Right. . . Absolutely. . . I know. . . Of course you are. . .Incredible ... Really? You want to be nice, pleasant, supportive. You want people to like you. So you agree with everything.
10. *Dreaming*—When we dream, we pretend to listen but really tune the other person out while we drift about in our interior fantasies. Instead of disciplining ourselves to truly concentrate on the input, we turn the channel to a more entertaining subject.
11. *Thinking speed*—Most of us speak between 60 to 180 words per minute, and people have capacity to think at the rate of 500 to 800 words per Minute. The difference leaves us with the great deal of mental spare time. While it is possible to use this time to explore the speaker's ideas, we most often let our mind wander to other matters - from the unfinished business just mentioned to romantic fantasies.
12. *Premature evaluation*—It often happens that we interrupt the speakers before they complete their thought, or finish their sentence, or state their conclusions. Directly as a result of our rapid

thinking speed, we race ahead of what we feel is the conclusion. We anticipate. We arrive at the concluding thought quickly although often that is quite different from what the speaker intended.

13. *Semantic stereotypes*—As certain kind of people bother us, so too do certain words. When these words are repeated time and again, they cause annoyance in the mind and effective listening is impaired.
14. *Delivery*—A monotonous delivery by the speaker can put listeners to sleep or cause them to loose interest.
15. *External distractions*—The entire physical environment effects the listening. Among the negative factors are noisy fans, poor or glaring lights, distracting background music, overheated or cold rooms, a conversation going on nearby, and so on.

APPROACHES TO LISTENING

Just as a carpenter or a chef uses different tools to tackle a job, listeners can take advantage of several skills for listening and responding to messages at work. Different approaches to listening are discussed below:

Passive listening—Sometimes the best approach to listening is to stay out of the way and encourage the speaker to keep going: "Uh-huh", "really", "Tell me more", and so on. Non-verbal cues like eye contact, attentive posture, and appropriate facial expressions are an important part of the passive listening. Generally this approach is used when there is one to one conversation or the speaker is giving a formal presentation.

Questioning—Sincere questions are genuine request for information: "when did you find that fuel was leaking from the barrel?", "When did you inform your manager?", and the like. These questions may be used to gather facts and details, clarify meanings, and encourage a speaker to elaborate.

Paraphrasing—Paraphrasing occurs when a listener restate the speaker's ideas in his own words in order to ensure that he has understood them correctly. This is often preceded by phrases such as, "Let me make sure I understand what you are saying...", "or "in other words you are saying..." and the like. We often think that we understand other person but we may be wrong at times. Paraphrasing is a practical technique that can highlight misunderstandings.

IMPROVING LISTENING SKILL

The ability to listen more effectively may be acquired through discipline and practice. As a listener you must be physically relaxed and mentally alert to receive and understand the message. Effective listening requires sustained concentration, attention to the main ideas presented, note-taking, and no emotional blocks to the message by the listener. You cannot listen passively and expect to retain the message. If you want to be an effective listener, you must give the communicator of the message sufficient attention and make an effort to understand his viewpoint. Here are some practical suggestions for effective listening, which, if followed, can appreciably increase the effectiveness of this communicative skill.

1. *Realise that listening is hard work*—You must appreciate the art of listening, and make conscious effort to listen others.
2. *Prepare to listen*—To receive the message clearly, the receiver must have the correct mental attitude. In your daily communications, establish a permissive environment for each communicator.

3. *Have positive attitude*—If you have to do it, do it with a positive attitude.
4. *Resist distractions*—Tune out internal and external distractions by facing and maintaining contact with the speaker. If you experience some negative environment factors, you can sometimes move to another location in the room. Good listeners adjust quickly to any kind of abnormal.
5. *Listen to understand, not refute*—Respect the viewpoint of those you disagree with. Try to understand the points they emphasize and why they have such feelings. Don't allow your personal biases and attitudes to influence your listening to the message.
6. *Keep an open mind*—A good listener doesn't feel threatened or insulted, or need to resist messages that contradict his beliefs, attitudes, ideas, or personal values. Try to identify and rationalise the words or phrases most upsetting to your means.
7. *Find an area of interest*—Good listeners are interested and attentive. They find ways to make the message relevant to themselves and/ or their jobs. Make your listening efficient by asking yourself 'what is he saying that I can use? Does he have any worthwhile ideas? Is he conveying any workable approaches or solutions? G. K Chesterton once said, "There is no such-thing as an uninteresting subject; there are only uninteresting people."
8. *Concentrate on the context*—Search out main ideas. Construct a mental outline of where speaker is going. Listen for transition and progression of ideas. If need be, you may reinforce the mental outline by physically taking down the notes.

9. *Capitalise on thought - speed*—Most of us think at about four times faster than the communicator speaks. It is almost impossible to slow down our thinking speed. What do you do with the excess thinking time while someone is speaking? The good listener uses thought-speed to advantage by applying spare thinking time to what is being said. Your greatest handicap may be not capitalising on thought-speed. Through listening training, it can be converted into your greatest asset.
10. *Combine verbal delivery with nonverbal cues*—The author of *Gestalt Theory Vibration*, said "Don't listen to the words just listen to what the voice tells you, what the movements tell you, what the posture tells you what the image tells you".
11. *Show some empathy*—Empathy means placing yourself in the shoes of speaker and try understand his viewpoint from there. If we show some empathy, we create a climate that encourages others to communicate honestly and openly. Therefore, try to see the communicator's point of view.
12. *Hold your fire*—Be patient. Don't interrupt. Don't become over-stimulated, too excited, or excited too soon, by what the speaker says. Be sure you understand what the speaker means; that is, withhold your evaluation until your comprehension is complete. Mentally arguing with a communicator is one of the principal reasons so little listening takes place in some discussions. Don't argue. If you win, you lose.
13. *Listen critically and delay judgement*—Good listeners delay making a judgement about the communicator's personality, the principal points of the message, and the response. Ask questions and

listen critically to the answers. Then, at the appropriate time, judgement can be passed in an enlightened manner.

TIPS TO BECOME BETTER LISTENER

Here are some hints and tips to make you a better listener:

1. Listen carefully to what the speaker says. Pick out the key words in any information. It's easier to remember one or two important words than a whole sentence. If you're taking a message for someone it's easier to write down key words to help you remember the message than it is to try to write everything out. You can add to your message after you've finished listening to the information.
2. Give each new stage in a set of instructions a number, it will help you remember them later.
3. Repeat the instructions or the information you've been given back to the person who gave them to you. If you've got anything wrong the person will correct you and the repetition will help you to remember.
4. Ask questions about anything that you are unsure of, or replay the recorded message.
5. Go through the complete sequence in your mind so that it is clear. If you're taking a message for someone else you might want to rewrite it using complete sentences so that it will make sense to the reader.
6. If you are with someone you need to do some extra things while you are listening, because you are part of a two-way process and you want to encourage the other person.

Look interested in what they are saying and maintain eye contact.

8. If the person is giving you directions, pay attention to the direction they are pointing. Gesture can be very important and can often make the speaker's meaning much clearer.

SECRETS TO LISTENING WELL

According to John Marshall, "Listening is as powerful a means of communication and influence as to talk well." There must be a lot of frustrated people out there, a lot of people who feel like they aren't listened to, a lot of people throwing up their arms and saying, "You just don't get it, do you?"

There seems to be a growing realisation of the importance of listening and communication skills in business. After all, lack of attention and respectful listening can be costly - leading to mistakes, poor service, misaligned goals, wasted time and lack of teamwork.

You can't sell unless you understand your customer's problem; you can't manage unless you understand your employee's motivation; and you can't gain team consensus unless you understand each team member's feelings about the issue at hand. In all of these cases, you must listen to others. However, listening is less important than how you listen. By listening in a way that demonstrates understanding and respect, you cause rapport to develop, and that is the true foundation from which you can sell, manage or influence others. "I like to listen. I have learned a great deal from listening carefully. Following are some keys to listening well:

— *Give 100% attention:* Prove you care by suspending all other activities.

- *Respond:* Responses can be both verbal and nonverbal but must prove you received the message, and more importantly, prove it had an impact on you. Speak at approximately the same energy level as the other person...then they'll know they really got through and don't have to keep repeating.
- *Prove understanding:* To say "I understand" is not enough. People need some sort of evidence or proof of understanding. Prove your understanding by occasionally restating the gist of their idea or by asking a question, which proves you, know the main idea. The important point is not to repeat what they've said to prove you were listening, but to prove you understand. The difference in these two intentions transmits remarkably different messages when you are communicating.
- *Prove respect:* Prove you take other views seriously. It seldom helps to tell people, "I appreciate your position" or "I know how you feel." You have to prove it by being willing to communicate with others at their level of understanding and attitude. We do this naturally by adjusting our tone of vice, rate of speech and choice of words to show that we are trying to imagine being where they are at the moment.

Listening to and acknowledging other people may seem deceptively simple, but doing it well, particularly when disagreements arise, takes true talent. As with any skill, listening well takes plenty of practice.

5

ART OF INTRAPERSONAL COMMUNICATION

The first step in achieving success in professional pursuits is mental preparation. We positively create our lives or we sabotage our lives. Most of us have associated sabotage with the act of undermining or backstabbing someone else. Truth sets you free—most individuals do more to undermine themselves than the combined efforts of everyone around them. The true sabotage lies within communication with oneself, in thoughts and words.

IMPROVING INTRAPERSONAL COMMUNICATION

Discipline of the Mind

The French philosopher Descartes was quoted as saying, "Except our own thoughts, there is nothing absolutely in our power." It is this power of thought that introduces the first step of the Communication Staircase. Intrapersonal Communication is the communication you have with yourself about yourself and others. It shares the inner workings of your mind with yourself. How often would you say you engage in mental chatter during the day? You talk to yourself more than you talk to anyone else. The important point is *how* you talk to yourself—what you say to yourself verbally and non-verbally.

Sizing up your internal communication is the first step, the basis of all other communication experiences within your work environment. It requires a lot of critical thought and awareness. When an individual pays serious attention to the daily conversations he has with himself, and critically examines the quality of experiences springing forth from these self-talks, he will be able to control more positively the materialisation of the experiences around him. I use this word "materialisation" literally. With our words we materialise the actions and events of our daily lives. You are either your greatest ally or your greatest adversary. We are all given the same empty screen as we start the *movie* of life. Then that screen fills with images and messages from our internal selves materialising into our external surroundings, including work. This ability to create our own movie, our own lives, is the gift and power shared by all humans.

Our thoughts and words are the tools of creation, our pens and brushes. The process of creation is based on the same pattern of materialisation shared by all species of creation. Specific conditions encourage creation. Seed + nutrient = tree. It is the same as Thought + word = action (or results). We create our lives with the brushstrokes of our thoughts and words! The Human Communication Cocreation Theory proposes that Conscious thoughts + words + feelings → subconscious = materialisation of life. The purpose of the subconscious is to accept something as true, then create it. That's why feelings play an important role. They generally do not lie. This knowledge is important to experiencing the type of work environment you are thriving in. The environment starts within you. Many of us can immediately identify our work environments as either positive or negative. But do you realise those labels come from inside you? Too often we look at either of these realms as being simply the result of someone else's actions or responsibility—our bosses, employees, co-workers, management. Not true. Your life starts and ends with you. Do others play a role in the environmental attitude? Of course they do, but only to the extent that you allow them. And yes, sometimes the organisational environment can be so toxic that the decision before you is whether to stay and tough it out or walk away and create a new situation. But before you throw in the towel, take a look at what you are adding to the communication environment of the organisation.

Dive into Your Life

Think of your life as a lake, a body of confined water. That which holds the lake in place—its banks, sediment, rocks, plants—represents your physical being, the body. The water in the lake represents your mind, your thoughts, the essence of your intellect or spirit that has no boundaries. Somehow the water, the internal you, continues to add to itself without ever overflowing its boundaries.

If I or someone else decided to fish in your lake on any given day at any given moment, what would we catch? Casting a rod into the depths of your mind would pull up what type of thoughts? When you go *fishing* into your own thoughts, second by second, what do you dredge up? How do you see yourself? What value do you place on yourself in comparison to others? Do you appreciate your coworkers? Do you respect your boss? Are you experiencing professional fulfilment at work?

Inside your *lake* are all the experiences and memories of your life. It is where you hold your values, attitudes, and beliefs. It is what houses that first birthday you remember, or your first kiss. It is that day at the park, or that first job and first promotion. It is also where you store the first harsh words you heard, the job you lost, emotional and physical abuse you suffered, the torment of bullies at school, the realisation of unfairness, the desire for acceptance, and the negative feelings of unrealised expectations. All the contents add up to the image you have of yourself. When you go *fishing,* which experiences are most likely to be reeled in? Probably those tied to your deepest desires or fears, the ones that have the greatest impact on how you see yourself. It is these experiences that create the image you call *you.* Your self-esteem and your self-worth come from the depth of these waters. Most of us can honestly say we do not have the cleanest, most pristine body of mental thoughts to fish from.

Your workplace personality is the mirror image of your self-image. It determines how you act in front of your coworkers and how you thrive and compete in the organisational culture.

When we communicate with others, we are bringing forth from our minds the reality created by us or for us, one that may be very different than the reality the coworker/listener is operating in. Think of the words in your vocabulary. Where did they come from? Who do they belong to? You? What if I told you that you do not own any words! None of the words you present with authority belong to you, nor were they devised by your incredible imaginations. When you were born, you were given a *platter of words* meant to define your specific circumstances of birth: male, female, black, white, cute, ugly, rich, poor, privileged, untouchable, and so on. As you moved through life, in and out of experiences, relationships, jobs, careers, you amassed more and more words and labels, claiming and accepting them as your own. Did you choose these words, these labels? No, you did not, but you did quickly agree and conform to them. We all did. We did not understand that, from the beginning of the process of enculturation, we had a choice. The Sapir-Whorf hypothesis is a linguistic "mould theory" that seeks to explain the impact of language on the individual, and how this impact, though very personal, is a shared experience for all humankind. In essence it states that language equals social reality. The words you use, most of them added to the language before you were born, have been assigned to you to define and determine how you should see and experience life.

For example, think about the many Inuit words for snow versus the absence of the same word/phenomenon in the world of the Maasai tribe of Kenya. Different realities create different degrees of relevance for different words. What type of reality do your words come from? What words have been assigned to you in the workplace: boss, supervisor, worker, CEO, janitor, secretary? What adjectives: smart, clever, persistent or lazy, dull?

Taking Ownership

We need to understand a fundamental truth concerning language: "He who owns the words, owns everything." As described before, on a platter before you are all the words you will need to fit into the prescribed place that society has already marked out for you. But you do not have the understanding to examine or question this platter; you just start eating. The feast includes all the words concerning your selfidentification —the way you see yourself and the manner in which you will live your life. The words describe your sex, gender, ethnicity, looks, social status, economics, opportunities, and so forth. No one cautions you to examine each word before you eat. Why not? Because they never examined the words put in front of them! Everyone around you is still absorbing the words on their platters, living up to the identities carved out for them. For far too many, these word choices are limiting, debilitating, and visionless.

You must take control over the words you use to create your daily images of self and others. I have examined the words presented to me on the platter of life and now am much more discerning about what I eat. If you do not take the time to define yourself, there are others lined up to do it for you. If you do not know who you are, there will be many others always ready to tell you *who you are not!* A famous quote by Winston Churchill best illustrates the power of being narrator of your own life: "History will be kind to me, for I intend to write it."

Behavioural Communication practitioners describe this process as *metacognition*—the ability to think about what you are thinking about. To cleanse your thoughts, you need to examine them. The work includes self-monitoring—the ability to watch your thoughts shape themselves, to understand how given thoughts will show up negatively or positively in your personal situation, and to deliberately choose to change course or move forward in the desired direction. This is a vital tool for understanding change as it happens in the moment. Too many of us go home from work and dredge up from our lake all the toxic waste of the workday, then spew it into the home environment.

Conquering the First Step

Lack of awareness and understanding is the first major obstacle to overcome. Once you are aware of the science of Intrapersonal Communication and understand its relationship to your life, you are ready to start the process of changing the world around you from inside out! And that start is where you stand right now. Individuals attempting to transform their lives by the renewing of their minds often feel overwhelmed by the task. Resist the urge to fall backward or leap ahead. Resist the temptation to dwell on the difficulties of reprogramming your thoughts. Replace the doubts of "can't do" with "can do" and "will do"! The power is within you to think what you want to think, not what others tell you to think or how others think. Do not fall into the trap of "this is too hard" or "I do not have the time." It is a matter of enjoying an abundant life or suffering an agonising, unfulfilled life!

First Things First

Start your day off the way you intend for it to go. As you begin to awaken while still lying quietly, purposefully greet the day with mental and verbal objectives, realistic expectations, and heartfelt thanksgivings. See yourself moving forward through your workday in the manner you wish to be received. Contemplate the attitude and actions you will exhibit as you think positively and constructively through your day *before* you hit the floor running. And there's another important point: stop running! It is the hurry-up attitude that has us all consistently scrambling away from where we are supposed to be—in the moment.

Personal responsibility for our own success and happiness is not a framework that is easy to work from in a world where what happens is too often everybody else's fault. Think about it. Are you both successful and happy? The wonderful writer and theologian Frederick Buechner shared with his students the formula for having a life of both success and happiness:

> "To find your mission in life is to discover the intersection between your heart's deep gladness and the world's deep hunger."

The first step is to understand the communication patterns that will positively affect every step you take thereafter. Below you will find a synopsis of how the first step of Intrapersonal Communication will help ensure your professional success and happiness.

Adopt these Intrapersonal Communication strategies throughout your communication workday:

- Understand how the *science* of communication goes far beyond an ability to talk.
  - With each thought, with each word, you create actions that turn into the life you are living.
- Understand that communication begins on the inside and determines the outside.
  - Take the first step to begin a new attitude of personal responsibility for the thoughts you are thinking. They cannot dwell there unless you invite them to stay.
- Clean out your lake—engage in a thorough examination of your thoughts and words and fill your lake with new agreements about yourself and others.
  - You must replace old doubts, fears, resentments, frustration, and anger with a renewed sense of self-worth, with self-love. Dr. Martin Luther King Jr. was quoted as saying, "No one can ride your back unless it is bent!" Straighten up!
  - Forgive yourself, forgive others, and move on up! Forgiveness allows you to remember the lesson without the anger or other negative emotions.

Use Affirmations, Meditation, Prayer

- Seek out pearls of wisdom and write them in a journal, on note cards, or in your Dreambook. Place the affirmations in locations where you will see and read them daily—the nightstand, your mirror, fridge, or desk. The wonderful thing about affirmations is they are there to confirm our dreams and goals. Don't just read them, but speak them aloud!

- Meditate on the vision you have for your life. Remember Descartes: "Except our own thoughts, there is nothing absolutely in our power." Think of your passion as if it already is!
- Prayer is a consistent conversation with that which is universal creativity.

Practice Self-monitoring

- As discussed earlier in the chapter, this Intrapersonal Communication tool allows you to be right there in the moment, involved in making choices as to your thoughts and resultant words. I cannot think of a more helpful tool to use at work. "Think before you speak!"

Practice Self-management

- As you enter your work environment, you immediately start to reaffirm the image you carry around of yourself at work. By understanding the connection between your external work environment and your internal processes of communication, you are assured of greater personal fulfilment and professional communication success.

Remember the lesson of "Be, Do, Have."

- Here's one approach to life: If I *have* a nice ride, I will *do* my thing by driving around town so everyone can see me, and then I will *be* somebody and everyone will know it.
- This formula bases self-worth in possessions. Self-esteem is replaced by social esteem.

— A better formula: If I (be) am successful in managing my mind, in choosing my thoughts and words, I will do things—make choices, take actions—that resonate with success. They will cause me to attract success and thereby have it. If I (be) am kind, I will do kind things and have kindness in return. The formula can be applied to millions of scenarios, but the outcome is always the same:

You have successfully begun your journey up the staircase by accepting the key part that self-understanding plays in your communication IQ. Our next step is to understand the role our non-verbal messages play in determining the outcome of our communication with others.

Do you realise that as much as 93 percent of your trust and believability is communicated through non-verbal communication?

6

EFFECTIVE NON-VERBAL COMMUNICATION

Non-verbal communication is strongly related to verbal communication. Nonverbal cues substitute for, contradict, emphasize, or regulate verbal messages. For instance, if someone asks us which way the rest-room is, we may simply point down the hall. We may compliment someone's new haircut while our faces give away the real feeling of dismay we have. We may describe a fish we caught with a motion of our hands to emphasize the monster-like proportions. And most certainly we regulate the flow of conversation non-verbally by raising an index finger, nodding and leaning forward, raising eyebrows, and/or changing eye contact.

STUDYING NON-VERBAL COMMUNICATION

Studying non-verbal communication presents a whole range of challenges that are unique to its nature. They include:

Non-verbal Cues can be Ambiguous

No dictionary can accurately classify them. Their meaning varies not only by culture and context, but by degree of intention, i.e., you may not be intending to communicate.

A random gesture may be assumed to have meaning when none at all was intended. Plus, some people who may feel emotion strongly nevertheless find that their bodies simply do not respond appropriately, i.e., someone who is feeling happy may not necessarily smile.

Non-verbal Cues are Continuous

This is practically related to the last point. It is possible to stop talking, but it is generally not possible to stop nonverbal cues. Also, spoken language has a structure that makes it easier to tell when a subject has changed, for instance, or to analyse its grammar. Non-verbal does not lend itself to this kind of analysis.

Non-verbal Cues are Multichannel

While watching someone's eyes, you may miss something significant in a hand gesture. Everything is happening at once, and therefore it may be confusing to try to keep up with everything. Most of us simply do not do so, at least not consciously. This has both advantages and disadvantages. Because we interpret non-verbal cues subconsciously and in a "right-brained", holistic fashion, it can happen quickly and fairly accurately. However, because it is not conscious and more "right-brained" it is difficult to put one's finger on exactly *why* one got a certain impression from someone, or even to put it into "left-brained" wording.

Non-verbal Cues are Culture-bound

Evidence suggests that humans of all cultures smile when happy and frown when unhappy. A few other gestures seem to be universal. However, most non-verbal symbols seem to be even further disconnected from any "essential meaning" than verbal symbols. Gestures seen as positive in one culture may be seen as obscene in another culture.

CATEGORIES OF NON-VERBAL COMMUNICATIONS

The major categories of nonverbal communications include the following:

personal space	eye contact	position
posture	paralanguage	expression
gesture	touch	locomotion
pacing	adornment	context
	physiologic responses	

Personal space: This category refers to the distance which people feel comfortable approaching others or having others approach them. People from certain countries, such as parts of Latin America or the Middle East often feel comfortable standing closer to each other, while persons of Northern European descent tend to prefer a relatively greater distance. Different distances are also intuitively assigned for situations involving intimate relations, ordinary personal relationships (e.g., friends), social relations (e.g., co-workers or salespeople), or in public places (e.g., in parks, restaurants, or on the street.)

Eye contact: This rich dimension speaks volumes. The Spanish woman in the Nineteenth Century combined eye language with the aid of a fan to say what was not permissible to express explicitly. Eye contact modifies the meaning of other non-verbal behaviours. For example, people on elevators or crowds can adjust their sense of personal space if they agree to limit eye contact. What happens if this convention isn't followed? This issue of eye contact is another important aspect of non-verbal communication. Modern American business culture values a fair degree of eye contact in interpersonal relations, and looking away is sensed as avoidance or even deviousness. However, some cultures raise children to minimise eye contact, especially with authority figures, lest one be perceived as arrogant or "uppity." When cultures interact, this inhibition of gaze may be misinterpreted as "passive aggressive" or worse.

Position: The position one takes vis-a-vis the other(s), along with the previous two categories of distance between people and angle of eye contact all are subsumed under a more general category of "proxemics" in the writings on non-verbal communications.

Posture: A person's bodily stance communicates a rich variety of messages. Consider the following postures and the emotional effect they seem to suggest:

slouching	stiff	slumped
twisted (wary)	cringing	towering
crouching	angled torso	legs spread
pelvis tilt	shoulders forward	general tightness
kneeling	angle of head	jaw thrust

Paralanguage: "Non-lexical" vocal communications may be considered a type of nonverbal communication, in its broadest sense, as it can suggest many emotional nuances. This category includes a number of sub-categories:

- Inflection (rising, falling, flat...)
- Pacing (rapid, slow, measured, changing...)
- Intensity (loud, soft, breathy,...)
- Tone (nasal, operatic, growling, wheedling, whining...)
- Pitch (high, medium, low, changes...)
- Pauses (meaningful, disorganised, shy, hesitant...)]

Facial Expression: The face is more highly developed as an organ of expression in humans than any other animal. Some of these become quite habitual, almost fixed into the chronic muscular structure of the face. For instance, in some parts of the South, the regional pattern of holding the jaw tight creates a slight bulge in the temples due to an overgrowth or "hypertrophy" of those jaw muscles that arise in that area. This creates a characteristic appearance. The squint of people who live a lot in the sun is another example. More transient expressions often reveal feelings that a person is not intending to communicate or even aware of. Here are just a few to warm you up:

pensive	amused	sad	barely tolerant
warning	pouting	anxious	sexually attracted
startled	confused	sleepy	intoxicated

Gesture: There are many kinds of gestures:

clenching fist	shaking a finger	pointing
biting fingernail	stugging at hair	squirming
rubbing chin	smoothing hair	folding arms
raising eyebrows	pursing lips	narrowing eyes
scratching head	looking away	hands on hips
hands behind head	rubbing nose	rocking
sticking out tongue	tugging earlobe	waving

These, too, have many different meanings in different cultures, and what may be friendly in one country or region can be an insult in another .

Touch: How one person touches another communicates a great deal of information: Is a grip gentle or firm, and does one hold the other person on the back of the upper arm, on the shoulder, or in the middle of the back. Is the gesture a push or a tug? Is the touch closer to a pat, a rub, or a grabbing? People have different areas of personal intimacy, and this refers not only to the sexual dimension, but also the dimension of self-control. Many adolescents are particularly sensitive to any touching that could be interpreted as patronising or undue familiarity. Even the angle of one's holding another's hand might suggest a hurrying or coercive implicit attitude, or on the other hand, a respectful, gentle, permission-giving approach.

Locomotion: The style of physical movement in space also communicates a great deal, as well as affecting the feelings of the person doing the moving

slither	crawl	totter	walk
stroll	shuffle	hurry	run
jog	spring	tiptoe	march
jump	hop	skip	climb
swing	acrobatics	swim	slink

Pacing: This is the way an action is done.

jerky	pressured	nervous	gradual
graceful	fatigued	tense	easy
shaky	deliberate	furtive	clumsy

A related variable is the time it takes to react to a stimulus, called "latency of response." Some people seem to react to questions, interact in conversations, or are slower or faster "on the uptake" than others.

Adornment: Our communications are also affected by a variety of other variables, such as clothes, makeup, and accessories. These offer signals relating to context (e.g. formal *vs.* informal), status, and individuality. The ways people carry cigarettes, pipes, canes, or relate to their belts, suspenders, or glasses also suggests different semiotic meanings.

Context: While this category is not actually a mode of nonverbal communication, the setting up of a room or how one places oneself in that room is a powerfully suggestive action. Where one sits in the group is often useful in diagnosing that person's attitude toward the situation. Group leaders need to be especially alert to the way the group room is organised. Consider the following variables and imagine how they might affect the interaction:

— amount and source of light

— colour of the lighting

- obvious props, a podium, blackboard
- the size of the room
- colours of the walls, floor, furniture
- seating arrangements
- number of people present
- environmental sounds, smells, and temperature
- the numbers and ratios of high-status and low status people
- the positioning of the various people in the space, who sits next to whom, who sits apart, who sits close, etc.

Physiological responses: This, too, is an exceptional category, because it cannot be practiced voluntarily. Still, it's useful for therapists and group members to become more aware of these subtle signs of emotion. It often helps to comment on these observations, as it implicitly gives permission to the person experiencing the emotion to more fully open to that feeling; or, sometimes, to more actively suppress it. Either way, the existence of that signal is made explicit in the group process. Some of the clues to physiological processes include:

shaking	flaring of nostrils	trembling chin
sweating	blanching	cold clammy skin
blushing	moisture in eyes	flushing
blinking	swallowing	breathing heavily

While a few of these behaviours can be mimicked, for the most part these reactions happen involuntarily. The only exercise is to watch for these reactions in oneself or others, at least mentally note their occurrence, and consider what the meaning of that emotional reaction might be.

INTERPRETING NON-VERBAL CUES

Immediacy

Immediacy cues communicate liking and pleasure. We move toward persons and things we like and avoid or move away from those we dislike. Generally, we instinctively decide whether we like someone or not and then later find "reasons" to back up our feelings. We can summarise the non-verbal behaviours then by saying that cues that move or lean or otherwise open up or go toward the other person communicate liking.

Cues that fall in this dimension include eye contact, mutual eye contact, touching, leaning forward, and touching.

Arousal

Arousal in this usage is similar to animation. That is, when we are interested in communicating with someone else, we tend to be more animated. A flat tone of voice and very little movement indicate a lack of interest.

Cues that fall in this dimension include eye contact, varied vocal cues, animated facial expressions, leaning forward, movement in general.

Dominance

These cues indicate something about the balance of power in a relationship. They communicate information about relative or perceived status, position, and importance. For instance, a person of high status tends to have a relaxed body posture when interacting with a person of lower status. High-status people tend to have more space around them, such as bigger offices, and more "barriers" such as more hallways, doors, and gatekeepers such as secretaries.

Furniture, clothing, and location also tend to communicate in this dimension.

IMPROVING NON-VERBAL COMMUNICATION

Check Context

Don't try to interpret cues isolated from other such cues, from the verbal communication, or from the physical or emotional context. As we've said in class, someone's arms being crossed may indicate nothing more than physical discomfort from a cold room.

Look for Clusters

This is the non-verbal context itself. See if the arms being crossed are accompanied by a resistance to eye contact and a flat tone of voice.

Consider Past Experience

We can more accurately interpret the behaviour of people we know. For one thing, we notice *changes* in behaviour more than the behaviour itself. Unless we know someone, we can't know that something has changed. For another thing, we interpret *patterns* of behaviour. Your mother may always cry when you come home from school with an A, and so you learn that this represent happiness in that particular situation.

Practice Perception Checking

This is basically the art of asking questions. For instance, you come home and announce to your significant other that you have received a great promotion that requires you to move to another state. Your announcement is met with silence. Rather than assume that s/he is upset, ask, "Does your silence mean that you're opposed to the move?" You may find out that s/he is simply stunned at the opportunity. Recognise that you are interpreting observed behaviour, not reading a mind, and check out your observation.

Ways to Improve your Non-verbal Communication

It is not only what you say in the classroom that is important, but it's how you say it that can make the difference to students. Non-verbal messages are an essential component of communication. Some major areas of nonverbal behaviours to explore are:

- Eye contact
- Facial expressions
- Gestures
- Posture and body orientation
- Proximity
- Paralinguistics
- Humour

Eye contact

Eye contact, an important channel of interpersonal communication, helps regulate the flow of communication. And it signals interest in others. Furthermore, eye contact with audiences increases the speaker's credibility. Teachers who make eye contact open the flow of communication and convey interest, concern, warmth and credibility.

Facial expressions

Smiling is a powerful cue that transmits:

- Happiness
- Friendliness
- Warmth

— Liking
— Affiliation

Thus, if you smile frequently you will be perceived as more likable, friendly, warm and approachable. Smiling is often contagious and students will react favourably and learn more.

Gestures

If you fail to gesture while speaking, you may be perceived as boring, stiff and unanimated. A lively and animated teaching style captures students' attention, makes the material more interesting, facilitates learning and provides a bit of entertainment. Head nods, a form of gestures, communicate positive reinforcement to students and indicate that you are listening.

Posture and Body Orientation

You communicate numerous messages by the way you walk, talk, stand and sit. Standing erect, but not rigid, and leaning slightly forward communicates to students that you are approachable, receptive and friendly. Furthermore, interpersonal closeness results when you and your students face each other. Speaking with your back turned or looking at the floor or ceiling should be avoided; it communicates disinterest to your class.

Proximity

Cultural norms dictate a comfortable distance for interaction with students. You should look for signals of discomfort caused by invading students' space. Some of these are:

— Rocking
— Leg swinging
— Tapping
— Gaze aversion

Typically, in large college classes space invasion is not a problem. In fact, there is usually too much distance. To counteract this, move around the classroom to increase interaction with your students. Increasing proximity enables you to make better eye contact and increases the opportunities for students to speak.

Paralinguistics

This facet of nonverbal communication includes such vocal elements as:

- — Tone
- — Pitch
- — Rhythm
- — Timbre
- — Loudness
- — Inflection

For maximum teaching effectiveness, learn to vary these six elements of your voice. One of the major criticisms is of instructors who speak in a monotone. Listeners perceive these instructors as boring and dull. Students report that they learn less and lose interest more quickly when listening to teachers who have not learned to modulate their voices.

Humour

Humour is often overlooked as a teaching tool, and it is too often not encouraged in college classrooms. Laughter releases stress and tension for both instructor and student. You should develop the ability to laugh at yourself and encourage students to do the same. It fosters a friendly environment that facilitates learning.

7

PRESENTATION SKILLS

A Presentation is a fast and potentially effective method of getting things done through other people. In managing any project, presentations are used as a formal method for bringing people together to plan, monitor and review its progress.

PURPOSE OF PRESENTATION

— *Firstly, it puts you on display.* Your staff needs to see evidence of decisive planning and leadership so that they are confident in your position as their manager. They need to be motivated and inspired to undertaking the tasks, which you are presenting.

Project leaders from other sections need to be persuaded of the merits of your project and to provide any necessary support. Senior management should be impressed by your skill and ability so that they provide the resources so that you and your team can get the job done.

— Secondly, it allows you to ask questions and to initiate discussion. It may not be suitable within the presentation formats of your company to hold a discussion during the presentation itself but it does allow you to raise the issues, present the problems and at least to establish who amongst the audience could provide valuable input to your decision-making.

- Presentations are your chance to speak your mind, to strut your stuff and to tell the people what the world is really like. While you hold the stage, the audience is bound by good manners to sit still and watch the performance.

A Good Presentation is an amalgamation of:

- *Content:* It contains information that you want to give and what the people need. Unlike reports, it must account for how much information the audience can absorb in one sitting.
- *Structure:* It has a logical beginning, middle, and end. It must be sequenced and paced so that the audience can understand it. The presenter must be careful not to loose the audience when wandering from the main point of the presentation.
- *Packaging:* One must remember that, the audience is at the mercy of a presenter.
- *Human element:* A good presentation will be remembered, because it has a person attached to it. But you still need to analyse the audience's needs very clearly.
- *The voice:* The voice is probably the most valuable tool of the presenter. It carries most of the content that the audience takes away. One of the oddities of speech is that we can easily tell others what is wrong with their voice, e.g. too fast, too high, too soft, etc., but we have trouble listening to and changing our own voices.
- *The volume:* How loud is the sound. The goal is to be heard without shouting. Good speakers lower

their voice to draw the audience in, and raise it to make a point.

- *Tone:* Often the tone enhances the effectivity of the meaning of a thought process. A voice that carries anger can annoy the audience, while a voice that carries humour can get the audience to feel good.
- *Pitch:* Pitch means how high or low a note is. Someone may have a high voice; some a moderate voice, while others may have a low voice.
- *Pace:* This is how long a sound lasts. Talking too fast causes the words and syllables to be short, while talking slowly lengthens them. Varying the pace helps to maintain the audience's interest line "This new dress code is going to be very formal" and saying it first with surprise, then with irony, then with grief, and finally with anger.

  The key is to over-act.

  Remember Shakespeare's words: "All the world's a stage"— presentations are the opening night on Broadway!
- *Eye contact:* Proper eye contact with each and everyone in the audience gives a sense of comfort to them and ensures that your convincing power becomes more effective.
- *Facial expressions:* A serious outlook, yet a little smile once in a while, results to a pleasant disposition and makes your audience more positively receptive to your presentation.
- *Practice:* Always practice the presentation that you have to deliver, beforehand, in front of your colleagues and at least once before a full length mirror. This is important as you can improve if you see your-self in the mirror, exactly the same manner other's would see you at a presentation.

There are two good methods for improving your voice:

- Listen to it! Practice listening to your voice while at home, driving, walking, etc.
- Then when you are at work or with company, monitor your voice to see if you are using it how you want to.

  To really listen to your voice, cup your right hand around your right ear and gently pull the ear forward. Next, cup your left hand around your mouth and direct the sound straight into your ear. This helps you to really hear your voice as others hear it...and it might be completely different from the voice you thought it was!
- Now practice moderating your voice.

OBJECTIVES OF COMMUNICATION

The single most important observation is that the objective of communication is not the transmission but the reception. The whole preparation, presentation and content of a speech must therefore be geared not to the speaker but to the audience.

The presentation of a perfect project plan is a failure if the audiences do not understand or are not persuaded of its merits. A customers' tour is a waste of time if they leave without realising the full worth of your product. The objective of communication is to make your message understood and remembered.

The main problem with this objective is, of course, the people to whom you are talking. The average human being has a very short attention span and many other things to think about.

Your job in the presentation is to reach through this mental fog and to hold the attention long enough to make your point and convince others in your favour..

It is difficult to over estimate the importance of careful preparation. Five minutes on the floor in front of senior management could decide the acceptance of a proposal of several months duration for the manager and the whole team.

With so much potential at stake, the presenter must concentrate not only upon the facts being presented but also upon the style, pace, tone and ultimately tactics, which should be used.

As a rule of thumb for an average presentation, no less than 1 hour should be spent in preparation for 5 minutes of talking.

How do you start?

Formulate your objectives

The starting point in planning any speech is to formulate a precise objective. This should take the form of a simple, concise statement of intent. For example, the purpose of your speech may be to obtain funds, to evaluate a proposal, or to motivate your team. No two objectives will be served equally well by the same presentation; and if you are not sure at the onset what you are trying to do, it is unlikely that your plan will achieve it.

Focus is key

If you do not focus upon your objective, it is unlikely that the audience will. In the end it is far more productive to achieve one goal than to blunder over several ones. The best approach is to isolate the essential objective and to list at most two others, which can be addressed providing they do not distract from the main one.

Identify the audience

The next task is to consider the audience to determine

how best to achieve your objectives in the context of these people. Essentially this is done by identifying their aims and objectives while attending your presentation. If you can convince them they are achieving those aims while at the same time achieving your own, you will find a helpful and receptive audience.

This principal of matching the audience aims, however, goes beyond the simple salesmanship of an idea – it is the simplest and most effective manner of obtaining their attention at the beginning. If your opening remarks imply that you understand their problem and that you have a solution, then they will be flattered at your attention and attentive to your every word.

Structure

All speeches should have a definite structure or format; a talk without a structure is a mess. If you do not organise your thoughts into a structured manner, the audience will not be able to follow them. Having established the aim of your presentation you should choose the most appropriate structure to achieve it. However, the structure must not get in the way of the main message. If it is too complex the audience will be distracted. If a section is unnecessary to the achievement of your fundamental objectives, pluck it out.

Sequential argument

One of the simplest structures is that of sequential argument which consists of a series of linked statements, ultimately leading to a conclusion. However, this simplicity can only be achieved by careful and deliberate delineation between each section. One technique is the use of frequent reminders to the audience of the main point, which have proceeded, and explicit explanation of how the next topic will lead on from this.

Hierarchical decomposition

In hierarchical decomposition the main topic is broken down into sub-topics and each sub-topic into smaller topics until eventually everything is broken down into very small basic units. In written communication this is a very powerful technique because it allows the reader to re-order the presentation at will, and to return to omitted topics at a later date. In verbal communication the audience is restricted to the order of the presenter and the hierarchy should be kept simple reinforced. As with sequential argument it is useful to summarise each section at its conclusion and to introduce each major new section with a statement of how it lies in the hierarchical order.

Question orientated

The aim of many presentations given by managers is to either explain a previous decision or to seek approval for a plan of action. In these cases, the format can be question orientated. The format is to introduce the problem and any relevant background, and then to outline the various solutions to that problem listing the advantages and disadvantages of each solution in turn. Finally, all possible options are summarised in terms of their pro's and con's, and either the preferred solution is presented for endorsement by the audience or a discussion is initiated leading to the decision. One trick for obtaining the desired outcome is to establish during the presentation the criteria by which the various options are to be judged; this alone should allow you to obtain your desired outcome.

Pyramid

Like in a newspaper, the story is introduced in its entirety in a catchy first paragraph. The next few paragraphs repeat the same information only giving further details to each point. The next section repeats the entire story again, but developing certain themes within each of the sub-points and again adding more information. This is repeated until the reporter runs out of story. The editor then simply decides upon the newsworthiness of the report and cuts from the bottom to the appropriate number of column inches.

There are two main advantages to this style for Presentations.

- Firstly, it can increase the audiences' receptiveness to the main ideas. Since at every stage of the pyramid they have all ready become familiar with the ideas and indeed know what to expect next. This sense of deja vu can falsely give the impression that what they are hearing are their own ideas.
- The second advantage is that the duration of the talk can be easily be altered by cutting the talk in exactly the same way as the newspaper editor might have done to the news story. This degree of flexibility may be useful if the same presentation is to be used several times in different situations.

The best bet

The simplest and most direct format remains the best bet. This is the simple beginning-middle-end format in which the main meat of the exposition is contained in the middle and is preceded by an introduction and followed by a summary and conclusion.

This is really the appropriate format for all small sub-sections in all the previous structures.

The beginning

It is imperative to plan your beginning carefully; there are six main elements:

(1) *Get their attention:* Too often, the first few minutes of the presentation are lost while people adjust their coats, drift in with coffee and finish the conversation they were having with the person next to them. You only have a limited time and every minute is precious to you so, from the beginning, make sure they pay attention. Start with a pleasant smile, a quick piercing eye-contact and a confident clear voice.

(2) *Establish a theme:* Basically, you need to start the audience thinking about the subject matter of your presentation. The audience will each have some experience or opinions on this and at the beginning you must make them bring that experience into their own minds.

(3) *Present a structure:* If you explain briefly at the beginning of a talk how it is to proceed, then the audience will know what to expect. This can help to establish the theme and also provide something concrete to hold their attention. Ultimately, it provides a sense of security in the promise that this speech too will end.

(4) *Create a rapport:* If you can win the audience over in the first few minutes, you will keep them for the remainder. You should plan exactly how you wish to appear to them and use the beginning to establish that relationship. You may be presenting yourself as their friend, as an expert, perhaps even as a judge, but whatever role you choose you must establish it at the very beginning.

(5) *Administration:* When planning your speech you should make a note to find out if there are any administrative details, which need to be announced at the beginning of your speech. This is not simply to make yourself popular with the people

organising the session but also because if these details are over looked the audience may become distracted as they wonder what is going to happen next.

(6) *The ending:* The final impression you make on the audience is the one they will remember. Thus it is worth planning your last few sentences with extreme care.

As with the beginning, it is necessary first to get their attention, which would have by now wandered. This requires a change of pace, a new visual aid or perhaps the introduction of one final culminating idea. In some formats the ending will be a summary of the main points of the talk. One of the greatest mistakes is to tell the audience that this is going to be a summary because at that moment they simply switch off. Indeed it is best that the ending comes unexpectedly with that final vital phrase left hanging in the air and ringing round their memories. Alternatively the ending can be a flourish, with the pace and voice leading the audience through the final crescendo to the inevitable conclusion.

(7) *Visual aids:* Most people expect visual reinforcement for any verbal message being delivered. While it would be unfair to blame television entirely for this, it is useful to understand what the audience is accustomed to. You will have to captivate the hearing as well as the eyesight of the audience to convince them in your favour. You can meet their expectations using a slide show, or even a video presentation. Do not clutter a view slide or it will confuse rather than assist. Do not place more data on the page than you wish to present.

(8) *The delivery:* Whatever you say and whatever you show in the slides, it is you, yourself which will remain the focus of the audience's attention. If you fret your hour upon the presentation stage, no-one will remember what you said.

The presenter has the power both to kill the message and to enhance it a hundred times beyond its worth.

KEY FACETS OF PRESENTATION SKILLS

Your job as a presenter is to use the potential of the presentation to ensure that the audience is motivated and inspired rather than disconcerted or distracted. Five key facets of presentation skills

- Eye contact
- The voice
- The facial expressions
- The overall physical appearance
- Body language

The Eyes

The eyes are said to be the key to the soul and are therefore the first and most effective weapon in convincing the audience of your honesty, openness and confidence in the objectives of your presentation.

Even when in conversation, your feelings can be evaluated by the intensity and duration of eye contact.

During the presentation you should use this to enhance your rapport with the audience by establishing eye contact with each and every member of the audience as often as possible.

For small groups this is clearly possible but it can also be achieved in large auditoriums since the further the audience is away from the presenter the harder it is to tell precisely where he or she is looking.

During presentations, try to hold your gaze fixed in specific directions for five or six seconds at a time. Shortly after each change in position, a slight smile will convince people in that direction that you have seen and acknowledged them.

The Voice

Two most important aspects of the voice for the public speaker are:

- Projection
- Variation

In ordinary conversation you can see from the expression, perhaps a subtle movement of the eye, when a word or phrase has been missed or misunderstood. In front of a bigger audience you have to make sure that this never happens. The simple advice is to slow down and to take your time. Remember the audience is constrained by good manners not to interrupt you so there is no need to maintain a constant flow of sound.

A safe style is to be slightly louder and slightly slower in the pace of delivery.

As you get used to the sound, you can adjust it by watching the audience. A monotone speech is boring, so it is important to try to vary the pitch and speed of your presentation. Similarly, Effective presentation in the English language is all about Stressing and Streching words, especially on those words or expressions that you want to emphasize more.

At the very least, each new sub-section should be proceeded by a pause and a change in tone to emphasize the delineation.

Expression

The audiences watch your face. If you are looking listless or distracted then they will be listless and distracted; if you are smiling, they will be wondering why and listen to find out. In normal conversation your meaning is enhanced by facial reinforcement. Thus in a speech you must compensate both for stage nerves and for the distance between yourself and the audience. Always remember that everyone wants to see a happy face, not a nervous one.

Appearance

There are many guides to management and presentation styles, which lay heavy emphasis upon the way you dress and in the last analysis this is a matter of personal choice. That choice should however be deliberately made. When you are giving a presentation you must dress for the audience, not for yourself; if they think you look out of place, then you are. A formal dress is what we would recommend. Ladies should not put too much make-up or jewellery.

Stance

When an actor initially learns a new character part, he or she will instinctively adopt a distinct posture or stance to convey that character. It follows therefore that while you are on stage, your stance and posture will convey a great deal about you. The least you must do is make sure your stance does not convey boredom; at best, you can use your whole body as a dynamic tool to reinforce your rapport with the audience.

Body Language

The problem is what to do with your hands. These must not wave aimlessly through the air, or fiddle constantly with a pen, or (worst of all visually) juggle change in your trouser pockets. The key is to keep your hands still, except when used in unison with your speech. To train them initially, find a safe resting place, which is comfortable for you, and aim to return them there when any gesture is completed. The best is to use both your hands in fine synchronisation, keep them above waist high and below your chest, so that they are visible by those looking at you. This shows that you are confident and it adds to your personality.

TECHNIQUES OF SPEECH

Every speaker has a set of "tricks of the trade" which he or she holds dear — the following are a short selection of such advice taken from various sources.

Make an Impression

The average audience is very busy: they have families, schedules and slippages, cars and mortgages; and although they will be trying very hard to concentrate on your speech, their minds will inevitably stray. Your job is to do something, anything, which captures their attention and makes a lasting impression upon them. Once you have planned your speech and honed it down to its few salient points, isolate the most important and devise some method to make it stick.

Repetition

The average audience is easily distracted, and their attention will slip during the most important message of your speech — so repeat it. You don't necessarily have to repeat a phrase, but simply make the point again and again and again with different explanations and in different ways.

Draw a Picture

The human brain is used to dealing with images, and this ability can be used to make the message more memorable. This means using metaphors or analogies to express your message. Thus a phrase like "we need to increase the market penetration before there will be sufficient profits for a pay related bonus" becomes "we need a bigger slice of the cake before the feast".

Jokes

The set piece joke can work very well, but it can also lead to disaster. You must choose a joke, which is apt, and one, which will not offend any member of the audience. This advice tends to rule out all racist, sexist or generally rude jokes. If this seems to rule out all the jokes you can think of, then you should avoid jokes in a speech.

Plain Speech

Keep it Simple, Short and Sweet

If you can crystallise your thoughts and combine your main message with some memorable phrase or imagery, and present them both in 30 seconds then you have either the perfect ending or the basis for a fine presentation.

Narrative

Everyone loves a story and stories can both instruct and convey a message. If you can weave your message into a story or a personal anecdote, then you can have them wanting to hear your every word - even if you have to make it up.

Practice

There is no substitute for rehearsal. You can do it in front of a mirror, or in front of your colleagues. In both cases, you should accentuate your gestures and vocal projection so that you get used to the sound and sight of yourself. Do not be put off by the mirror - remember: you see a lot less of yourself than what the others do.

Relaxation

If you get nervous just before the show, either concentrate on controlling your breathing. The good news is that the audience will never notice your nerves nearly as much as you think.

Similarly, if you dry-up in the middle — smile, look at your notes, and take your time. The silence will seem long to you, but less so to the audience.

Evaluate

Once the speech is over and you have calmed down, you should try to honestly evaluate your performance. Either alone, or with the help of a friend in the audience, decide what was the least successful aspect of your presentation and resolve to concentrate on that point in the next talk you give. If it is a problem associated with the preparation, then deal with it there; if it is a problem with your delivery, write yourself a reminder note and put it in front of you at the next talk. Practice is only productive when you make a positive effort to improve — try it.

To Wrap it Up

The material of your presentation should be concise, to the point and tell an interesting story. In addition to the obvious things like content and visual aids, the following are just as important as the audience will be subconsciously taking them in:

Your voice - how you say it is as important as what you say.

Body language - Your body movements express what your attitudes and thoughts really are.

Appearance - First impressions influence the audience's attitudes to you.

Dress appropriately for the occasion, in formals.

As with most personal skills oral communication cannot be taught. Instructors can only point the way. So as always, practice is essential, both to improve your skills generally and also to make the best of each individual presentation you make.

Preparation

(1) Prepare the structure of the talk carefully and logically, just as you would for a written report. What are:
  - The objectives of the talk?
  - The main points you want to make?
  - Make a list of these two things as your starting point

(2) Write out the presentation in rough, just like a first draft of a written report. Review the draft. You will find things that are irrelevant or superfluous - delete them. Check the story is consistent and flows smoothly. If there are things you cannot easily express, possibly because of doubt about your understanding, it is better to leave them unsaid.

(3) Never read from a script. It is also unwise to have the talk written out in detail as a prompt sheet - the chances are you will not locate the thing you want to say amongst all the other text.

You should know most of what you want to say - if you don't then you should not be giving the talk! So prepare cue cards, which have key words and phrases on them. Postcards are ideal for this. Don't forget to number the cards in case you drop them.

(4) Remember to mark on your cards the visual aids that go with them so that the right Overhead Projection or slide is shown at the right time

(5) Rehearse your presentation - to yourself at first and then in front of some colleagues. The initial rehearsal should consider how the words and the sequence of visual aids go together. How will you make effective use of your visual aids?

MAKING THE PRESENTATION

(1) Greet the audience, and tell them who you are.

(2) Tell the audience what you are going to tell them.

(3) At the end tell them what you have told them

(4) Stick to the time limit. If you can, keep it short. It's better to under-run than over-run. As a rule of thumb, allow 2 minutes for each general overhead transparency or Power Point slide you use, but longer for any that you want to use for developing specific points.

(5) The audience will get bored with something on the screen for more than 5 minutes, especially if you are not actively talking about it. So switch the display off, or replace the slide with some form of 'wallpaper' such as a company logo.

(6) Stick to the plan for the presentation, don't be tempted to digress - you will eat up time and could end up in a dead-end with no escape!

(7) Unless explicitly told not to, leave time for discussion - 5 minutes is sufficient to allow clarification of points. The session chairman may extend this if the questioning becomes interesting.

(8) At the end of your presentation ask if there are any questions - avoid being tense when you do this as the audience may find it intimidating

(9) If questions are slow in coming, you can start things off by asking a question of the audience - so have one prepared.

Delivery

— Speak clearly. Don't shout or whisper - judge the acoustics of the room.

— Don't rush, or talk deliberately slowly. Be natural and preferably conversational maintaining a steady pace of delivery.

— Deliberately pause at key points - this has the effect of emphasizing the importance of a particular point you are making.

— Avoid jokes - unless you are a natural expert to being a professional flirting or light hearted humour.

— Use your hands to emphasize points but don't indulge in too much hand waving. People can, over time, develop irritating habits. Ask colleagues occasionally what they think of your style.

— Look at the audience as much as possible, but don't fix on an individual - it can be intimidating or lead to misunderstanding.

— Pitch your presentation towards the back of the audience, especially in larger rooms.

- Don't face the display screen behind you and talk to it.

Other annoying habits include:

- Standing in a position where you obscure the screen. In fact, positively check for anyone in the audience who may be at a disadvantage and try to accommodate them.
- Muttering over a transparency on the OHP projector plate and not realising that you are blocking the projection of the image. It is preferable to point to the screen than the foil on the OHP
- Avoid moving about too much. Pacing up and down can unnerve the audience, although some animation is desirable.
- Keep an eye on the audience's body language. Know when to stop and also when to cut out a piece of the presentation.
- Visual aids must be relevant to what you want to say. A careless design or use of a slide can simply get in the way of the presentation. What you use depends on the type of talk you are giving. Here are some possibilities:
  - Overhead projection transparencies (OHPs) on 35 mm slides
  - Computer projection (Power point , applications such as Excel, etc)
  - Video, and film,
  - Real objects - either handled from the speaker's bench or passed around
  - Flipchart or blackboard/white board - possibly used as a 'scratch-pad' to expand on a point

- Keep it simple though - a complex set of hardware can result in confusion for speaker and audience.
- Make sure you know in advance how to operate an equipment and also when you want particular displays to appear. Sometimes a technician will operate the equipment.
- Arrange beforehand what is to happen and when and what signals you will use.
- Edit your slides as carefully as your talk - if a slide is superfluous then leave it out.
- Slides and OHPs should contain the minimum information necessary. The contents should be used more as references for your presentation as well as for your audience.

  To do otherwise, risks the slide being unreadable or will divert your audience's attention so that they spend time reading the slide rather than listening to you.
- Try to limit words per slide to a maximum of 10.
- Use a reasonable size font and a typeface, which will enlarge well. Typically use a minimum 16 - 18 Times Roman/Arial on OHPs.
- A guideline is: if you can read the OHP from a distance of 2 metres (without projection) then it's probably OK.
- Avoid using a diagram prepared for a technical report in your talk. It will be too detailed and difficult to read.
- Do not use colours in your slides except for visuals. Even for visuals, avoid orange and

yellow which do not show up very well when projected.

— For text only, white on black is pleasant and clear to look at and easy to read.

— Room lighting should be considered. Too much light near the screen will make it difficult to see the detail. On the other hand, a completely darkened room can send the audience to sleep.

— Try to avoid having to keep switching lights on and off, but if you do have to do this, know where the light switches are and how to use them.

8

INTERNAL COMMUNICATIONS

Internal communications includes all communication within an organisation. Communication may be oral or written, face to face or virtual, one-on-one or in groups. Effective internal communication is a vital means of addressing organisational concerns. Clear and concise internal communication helps to establish formal roles and responsibilities for employees and maintain organisation and clarity within an establishment.

Internal communication involves the communication that exists within a company and can take many forms. Key to the success of an organisation is communication from within. In order to effectively engage in two-way symmetrical communication, communication is essential internally. Adaptability to changes that occur external from an organisation stems from knowingness of efficient usage of communication internally.

Internal communications helps employees to understand the organisation's vision, values and culture. It may involve staff members in issues that affect working life and keeps staff informed on important decisions taken by management. Furthermore, when implemented effectively, it can be crucial in a time of crisis, providing employees with not only a strategy to handle a crisis, but the facts surrounding such an event.

As arguably some of the most invested individuals in an organisation, trusted and valued employees can prove to be excellent partners when addressing a crisis. By maintaining open lines of communication between management and employees, effective internal communications can enhance stronger relationships throughout all levels of the organisation and forge a sense of community.

Excellent internal communications cannot simply be implemented and left alone; the process must be ever-changing and adaptable for success. While more and more organisations begin to spend more time identifying special interest groups within their own walls, internal communications methods are becoming increasingly diverse to match the varying needs of each organisations' internal staff and stakeholders.

COMMON CAUSES OF PROBLEMS IN INTERNAL COMMUNICATIONS

1. "If I know it, then everyone must know it." Perhaps the most common communications problem is managements' assumption that because they are aware of some piece of information, than everyone else is, too. Usually staff isn't aware unless management makes a deliberate attempt to carefully convey information.
2. "We hate bureaucracy-we're 'lean and mean.'" When organisations are just getting started, their leaders can often prize themselves on not being burdened with what seems as bureaucratic overhead, that is, as extensive written policies and procedures. Writing something down can be seen as a sign of bureaucracy and to be avoided. As the organisation grows, it needs more communications and feedback to remain healthy, but this

communication isn't valued. As a result, increasing confusion ensues — unless management matures and realises the need for increased, reliable communications.

3. "I told everyone or some people, or ...?" Another frequent problem is managements' not really valuing communications or assuming that it just happens. They are not aware of what they told to whom-even when they intended for everyone to know the information.
4. "Did you hear what I meant for you to hear?" With today's increasingly diverse workforce, it's easy to believe you've conveyed information to someone, but you aren't aware that they interpreted you differently than you intended. Unfortunately, you won't be aware of this problem until a major problem or issue arises out of the confusion.
5. "Our problems are too big to have to listen to each other." Particularly when personnel are tired or under stress, it's easy to do what's urgent rather than what's important. So people misunderstand others' points or understand their intentions. This problem usually gets discovered too late, too.
6. "So what's to talk about?" Lastly, communications problems can arise when inexperienced management interprets its job to be solving problems and if they're aren't any problems/crises, then there's nothing that needs to be communicated.
7. "There's data and there's information." As organisations grow, their management tends to focus on matters of efficiency. They often generate systems that produce substantial amount of data-raw information that doesn't seem to really be important.

8. "If I need your opinion, I'll tell it to you." Lastly, communications problems can arise when management simply sees no value whatsoever in communicating with subordinates, believing subordinates should just do their jobs.

ASPECTS OF GOOD INTERNAL COMMUNICATIONS

Internal communication should be:

- Transparent and timely (when details have been confirmed and approved, messages should be presented to employees before any external public)
- Clear
- Concise
- Informative
- Independent
- Relevant
- Compelling

Internal communications practitioners should adhere to certain values such as:

- Openness
- Honesty
- Two-way symmetrical communication

Internal Communication enables change and allows 'transfer of meaning'.

PRINCIPLES TO EFFECTIVE INTERNAL ORGANISATIONAL COMMUNICATIONS

1. Unless management comprehends and fully supports the premise that organisations must have high degrees of communications, the organisation will remain stilted. Too often, management learns

the need for communication by having to respond to the lack of it.

2. Effective internal communications start with effective skills in communications, including basic skills in listening, speaking, questioning and sharing feedback. These can developed with some concerted review and practice. Perhaps the most important outcome from these skills is conveying that you value hearing from others and their hearing from you.
3. Sound meeting management skills go a long way toward ensuring effective communications, too.
4. A key ingredient to developing effective communications in any organisation is each person taking responsibility to assert when they don't understand a communication or to suggest when and how someone could communicate more effectively.

Internal Communications Departments

An internal communications department can become a moderator of interaction between official organisational representatives and employees.

The internal communications department should be responsible for developing and maintaining a number of channels that allow effective communication to take place. These channels include:

- Intranet Web Site
- An informal session where employees can listen to and talk with the organisational representative such as a managing director, such as a Town Meeting
- Conference calls

- Internal newsletters/ brochures/ other printed, tangible materials
- E-mail
- Message boards
- Personal or group meetings
- Virtual meetings

IMPORTANCE OF INTERNAL COMMUNICATION

Internal communication is considered a vital tool for binding an organisation, enhancing employee morale, promoting transparency and reducing attrition. Ironically, while everybody understands and talks about the significance of internal communication, very few are able to manage it efficiently. Both the long-term and short-term fallout of ineffective internal communication can be damaging for an organisation. It can start from the spread of rumours to disillusionment among employees to a gradual destruction of the company's brand image. Worse, it may also lead to the slow death of the organisation.

9

BUSINESS LETTER WRITING

The business letter is the basic means of communication between two companies. It is estimated that close to 100 million Business Letters are written each day. It is a document typically sent externally to those outside a company but is also sent internally to those within a company. Most business letters have a formal tone. You should write a business letter whenever you need a permanent record that you sent the information enclosed. Because you generally send business letters to other professionals, always include a formal salutation and closing.

PURPOSE OF A BUSINESS LETTER

You will write business letters to inform readers of specific information. However, you might also write a business letter to persuade others to take action or to propose your ideas. Business letters even function as advertisements at times. Consider the letters long-distance phone companies send to those not signed up for their services or the cover letter to your resume. Both of these serve to promote or advertise. Business letters can be challenging to write, because you have to consider how to keep your readers' attention. This is particularly the case if your readers receive large amounts of mail and have little time to read.

Writing business letters is like any other document: First you must analyse your audience and determine your purpose. Then you gather information, create an outline, write a draft, and revise it. The key to writing business letters is to get to the point as quickly as possible and to present your information clearly.

GENERAL FORMAT

When you write a business letter, you will follow a general format. However, your company may have specific requirements that you must use. For instance, a company might have a particular way of presenting a salutation or may even use a specific type of letterhead. Because a business letter is an effective way to communicate a message, its format should allow readers to quickly grasp information. Information should stand out to readers as they scan the document. Remember, a business letter reflects your professionalism.

- Heading or Return Address
- Inside Address
- Attention Line
- Subject Line
- Salutation
- Body
- Complimentary Close and Signature
- Reference and Enclosure Lines
- Copy Line

Letterhead or Return Address

Readers should always be able to quickly locate your contact information. This information is located at the top of the business letter in the return address or by using the company's letterhead. This includes:

- Name
- Address
- Phone number
- Company logo or letterhead

The letterhead and the date the letter will be sent make up the heading. When printing on blank paper, use your address and date as the heading.

Inside Address

The inside address is your reader's full address. This includes the reader's:

- Name
- Position
- Organisation
- Complete mailing address

If your reader has a courtesy title, such as Professor or Doctor then use it. Otherwise use Mr. or Ms., unless you know the reader prefers Miss or Mrs. These should also appear identically on the envelope.

Attention Line

When you cannot address a business letter to a particular person, use an attention line:

Attention: Human Resource Manager

Use the attention line if you want an organisation to respond even if the person you write to is unavailable. In this instance, put the name of the organisation or division on the first line of the inside address, and the attention line immediately afterwards:

Subject Line

Use a brief phrase or keywords to describe the content of the business letter:

Body

The body of a business letter is typically single-spaced and has three paragraphs:

- Introductory paragraph
- One or more body paragraphs
- Concluding paragraph

Like essays written for college courses, a business letter introduces one main idea and then supports this idea. At the end of the letter, always include a way for your readers to contact you. Finally, consider how your letter looks. If you have nothing but paragraph after paragraph of text, you might use lists to draw attention to specific information. Lists are effective ways to present information because they break down large amounts of text and are visually pleasing. Lists are especially useful when you have to convey steps, phases, years, procedures, or decisions, and can be bulleted or numbered.

When creating a list, consider writing phrases, fragments or even questions and answers. By avoiding full sentences in a list, your information is concise and more likely to engage your readers. For example, to receive a degree in engineering, you must complete the following:

- Core Courses
- Elective Courses
- Senior Design

Complimentary Close and Signature

Business letters should end with a closing, such as:

— Sincerely,

— Cordially,

— Best regards,

— Yours very truly,

Capitalise only the first word in the complimentary close, and follow all phrases with a comma.

You should also remember to sign and type your name under the closing.

End Notations

If someone else types your letters, the reference line identifies this person, usually by initials. It appears a few spaces below the signature line, along the left margin. The writer's initials come first, and they are capitalised.

NS/AS.

If the envelope contains any documents other than the letter itself, identify the number of enclosures:

— Enclosure or

— Enclosure (1), which means two documents

In determining the number of enclosures, count only the separate items, not the number of pages.

Copy Line

The copy line is used to let the reader know that other people are receiving a copy of the document. Use the following symbols:

— c: for copy

— pc: for photocopy

— bc: blind copy

Follow the symbol with the names of the other recipients, listed either alphabetically or according to organisational rank. If you do not want your reader to know about the other copies, type bc on the copies only, not the original.

Effective Writing

Even though no one formula exists for a perfect business letter, some basic guidelines will help you, regardless of the form, purpose, and audience of the document. Many executives still prefer a written document over other forms of communication, because the document can serve as a contract, the facts will be on record in writing, and executives do not have to rely on memory.

This is why it is important to write a good Business Letter, and the principles below will help you to do so.

- Empathy
- Persuasion
- Tone
- Service Perspective

Empathy

Empathy means to care about someone's feelings or ideas. A well-written business letter will convey the feeling that the writer does care about the reader and is genuinely interested in working together to solve a problem or discuss a concept. To write a good letter, put yourself in the reader's shoes and try to anticipate the reader's reaction to your comments. By doing this, you are more likely to choose more appropriate words and use the correct tone.

Persuasion

Every business letter is in some degree a sales letter, because you are always requesting a response or course of action. Therefore, the following principles of persuasion will help you compose and efficient and effective Business Letter:

- Plan according to the reader's reaction
- Write with the "you" attitude- the state of mind where you always emphasize the benefits to the reader and subordinate your interests. This can be accomplished by using empathy and the words "you" and "your" often
- Adjust the language to the reader and use terms and concepts that the reader is familiar with
- Write positively and with confidence.

Tone

Tone is the use of accent and inflection to express a mood or emotion in speaking or writing. Many times it is not what you say in a business letter, but how you say it. It is a good idea to always consider your tone so that you do not risk upsetting the reader, thereby lessening the chances your requests and comments will be respected.

You can avoid making mistakes with tone by using the following techniques:

- Avoid the "I" attitude by having more emphasis on the reader and not yourself.
- Avoid extreme cases of humility, flattery, and modesty.
- Avoid condescension.
- Avoid preaching your ideas.

TYPES OF BUSINESS LETTERS

The following are the most common types of business letters. Keep in mind that the purpose and audience of your business letter effects, which form you, choose.

- The Acknowledgement letter
- The Inquiry letter

- Response to an inquiry letter
- Complaint letter
- Order letter

Acknowledgement Letters

A letter of acknowledgement is good public relations manoeuvre. Though not always required, they can go along way. Remember, it's the thought that counts. The objective is to let the reader know you are in receipt of whatever it is was they sent; usually something requested in an inquiry letter. It can be viewed as a response to a response. The actual scope of an acknowledgement letter need only include a small detail, such as what day something arrived, and an expression of appreciation. It's most important function is to say thank you, a mark of professional courtesy. In the sample acknowledgement letter the writer confirms receipt of information and appreciates the sender's promptness. She also references a specific point to which she is sure to return in an as yet, unscheduled appointment. Here are the steps to follow when writing an acknowledgement letter. Each link provides tips and a blank editing box in which you can practice your writing skills. You will be able to save and edit the contents of these boxes while working on your writing project.

- Identify your reader.
- Establish your objective.
- Determine your scope.
- Organise your letter.
- Draft your letter
- Close your letter
- Review and revise your letter

Identify Your Reader

The identity of the reader to whom you are sending an acknowledgement will be found in the complimentary close of a previous response letter. That person's name should be placed in the salutation and the inside heading of your reply. It should also be included on the top line of your envelope. Remember that people do business with people first, businesses second. When you address your reader by name, you are recognising their individual importance, their value as a human being. In the inside heading of the sample acknowledgement letter the reader is identified by both his name and the position he holds.

Establish Your Objective

The objective of an acknowledgement letter is to let the reader know you are in receipt of whatever it is was that you requested. You should be brief.

In the body of the sample acknowledgement letter, the writer mentions a specific point, clarifying for the reader that it is an important part of her overall objective, letting him know that further discussion will be expected in their upcoming meeting. Briefly mention what you have received, when you received it and that you appreciate the senders effort.

Determine Your Scope

The scope of an acknowledgement letter encompasses very little. It provides the reader with a short line or two, the objective of which is to notify that a request has been satisfied. Should it be useful, the scope may be broadened to include new information, particularly if a continuing dialogue is desired. In the body of the sample acknowledgement letter the writer provides the name of her assistant, a second contact person with whom he can speak should he/she be unavailable to take his call. This establishes a line of communication that indicates her serious interest in exploring a further business relationship. Make a simple list of what you want to tell your reader.

Organise Your Letter

Organising an acknowledgement letter is a simple procedure designed to help you draft your request. You have established your objective and determined the scope. Refer back to them. Together they make up the main components in the body of your letter.

A simple outline will get you organised. A list will probably do the job. Consider each item on the list as having a logical place, either at the beginning, the middle or the end of your letter. Put each item where it belongs.

With list in hand you can begin a rough draft. Most of your thinking is done and you can concentrate on the writing task. You won't be worried about forgetting something important. It's already on your list. You won't be worried about in what order things should appear. Your list is already organised. When you begin the rough draft your outline will become a checklist.

Draft Your Letter

Working from an outline is the simplest way to draft a adjustment letter. Refer back to your list and turn each fragmentary sentence into a full and complete sentence expressing a single thought or idea.

Concentrate on communicating your objective to your reader. Be certain that you describe the scope of your solution with an appropriate amount of information.

Keep in mind that you are writing a rough draft. For an overall sense of cohesion, be as quick as you can.

Spelling, grammar, sentence and paragraph structure need not be perfect. Those details will be tuned up in the final step when you review and revise your work.

Start with the point that you feel the strongest or most confident about and then do the others. Remember to do this quickly. On completion you will have a rough draft that can be saved and edited.

Do one at a time, starting with the point that you are most confident about turning into a complete sentence. Then do the others. Remember, it is best to do this quickly. On completion you will have a rough draft that can be saved and edited.

Close Your Letter

An acknowledgement letter should close with a professional tone and style. Once your last paragraph is written, sign off between a complimentary close such as "Sincerely" or "Thank you," and your printed name.

If your acknowledgement letter is written in conjunction with an official duty, place your title below the printed name as in the sample acknowledgement letter. Additional information such as dictation remarks, notification of attachments and copies sent to other individuals should be placed beneath your title line. In situations where you are unsure of the proper close, consult the Formatting Business Letters page for acceptable options.

Review and Revise Your Letter

Reviewing and revising your acknowledgement letter is the final step in the writing process. You will check your draft in this step, making sure that your objective is clear and your scope is concise. Put yourself in the reader's shoes as you examine the rough draft. Ask yourself, as the recipient, whether you are able to comprehend the request quickly and if enough information has been included to enable a timely response.

Look for the obvious errors first. Check for spelling, sentence structure and grammar mistakes. Remember that a passive voice is not as commanding as an active one. You want your inquiry to be strong, so write with an active voice.

The important thing to keep in mind is the overall cohesiveness of the whole unit. Look for accuracy, clarity and a sense of completeness. Ask yourself if the transitions between paragraphs are working and if your point of view, tone and style are consistent throughout the text.

Examine your word choices carefully. Ambiguous words lead to confusion. Jargon and abstract terms may not be understood at all and affectations, clichés and trite language serve no real purpose and will obscure your objective. You want to help your reader understand exactly what it is that you want, so remove all that is not helpful.

And finally, if you have not written an opening or a conclusion now is the time. The introduction needs to lead into the body of your letter with a firm statement about the subject of your inquiry and enough supporting information to keep the reader reading. Your closing remarks need to reiterate your objective with a question that calls for an action.

Complaint Letters

A complaint letter, also known as a claim, advises a business that an error has been made or that a defect has been discovered. The objective is to provide detailed information regarding the error or defect. It also serves as a legal document notifying the recipient that a correction or adjustment is being requested.

Keep in mind that your reader is most likely a trained customer service professional and not the person responsible for the error or defect. Rather than being angry, use a firm but courteous tone when stating your complaint. Remember, it is results you are after.

The scope of a complaint letter should include only the relevant facts validating your claim and a request that appropriate corrective steps be taken. The scope may also detail the options that you are willing to accept in satisfaction of the claim. In the sample complaint letter the writer explains that an incorrect shipment was received and that a promised correction has not materialised. He then proposes two equally satisfactory solutions.

— Identify your reader.

— Establish your objective.

— Determine your scope.

— Organise your letter.

— Draft your letter

— Close Your letter

— Review and revise your letter

Identify Your Reader

Although a clearly identified reader is not absolutely necessary, a complaint letter should be addressed to the person who is most able to resolve an unsatisfactory situation. In a very small business the owner is generally the contact person. In a mid-size company a vice president or upper level management person solves problems. Large companies often have a Customer Service department to whose attention a complaint can be addressed. In these cases, the inside heading should contain just the name and address of the company. The salutation will then be replaced by a simple attention getting device such as that shown in the sample complaint letter.

Establish Your Objective

The objective of a complaint letter is to prompt an action that resolves a conflict. You should avoid threats and accusations when providing the details of your complaint. Stick to the facts and your reader will comprehend what went wrong and what action you expect to have implemented.

Any company or business organisation with a legitimate complaint lodged against them will act quickly to resolve the problem. Doing so fulfills a primary business goal: keeping the customer satisfied. In the first sentence of the sample complaint letter, the writer clearly states that he has received an incorrectly filled order, establishing legitimate grounds for both his complaint and request for corrective action.

Determine Your Scope

The scope of a complaint letter should encompass the relevant information necessary to resolve a problem, correct an error or repair a defect. It should provide the reader with exact descriptions, including dates, times and places. It should reference purchase orders, invoice numbers, payment records and even dollar amounts when appropriate.

In the body of the sample complaint letter the writer politely expresses dissatisfaction that a problem's promised resolution is long overdue. He supports his claim with facts. Make a simple list of your complaints. Be specific. Attention to detail is very important. Feel free to delete or add items. You can save and edit this list as you work. On completion you will have determined your scope.

Organise Your Letter

Organising a complaint letter is a simple procedure designed to help you draft your request. You have already started this task. You have established your objective and determined the scope. Refer back to them. Together they make up the main components in the body of your letter.

A simple outline will get you organised. A list will probably do the job. Consider each item on the list as having a logical place, either at the beginning, the middle or the end of your letter. Put each item where it belongs.

With list in hand you can begin a rough draft. Most of your thinking is done and you can concentrate on the writing task. You won't be worried about forgetting something important. It's already on your list. You won't be worried about in what order things should appear. Your list is already organised.

When you begin the rough draft your outline will become a checklist.

Draft Your Letter

Working from an outline is the simplest way to draft a adjustment letter. Refer back to your list and turn each fragmentary sentence into a full and complete sentence expressing a single thought or idea.

Concentrate on communicating your objective to your reader. Be certain that you describe the scope of your solution with an appropriate amount of information.

Keep in mind that you are writing a rough draft. For an overall sense of cohesion, be as quick as you can. Spelling, grammar, sentence and paragraph structure need not be perfect. Those details will be tuned up in the final step when you review and revise your work.

Start with the point that you feel the strongest or most confident about and then do the others. Remember to do this quickly. On completion you will have a rough draft that can be saved and edited.

Do one at a time, starting with the point that you are most confident about turning into a complete sentence. Then do the others. Remember, it is best to do this quickly. On completion you will have a rough draft that can be saved and edited.

Close Your Letter

A complaint letter should close with a professional tone and style. Once your last paragraph is written, sign off between a complimentary close such as "Sincerely" or "Thank you," and your printed name.

If your credit letter is written in conjunction with an official duty, place your title below your printed name as shown in sample complaint letter. Additional information such as dictation remarks, notification of enclosures and copies sent to other individuals should be placed beneath your title line. In situations where you are unsure of the proper close, consult the Formatting Business Letters page for acceptable options.

Review and Revise Your Letter

Reviewing and revising your complaint letter is the final step in the writing process. You will check your draft in this step, making sure that your objective is clear and your scope is concise. Put yourself in the reader's shoes as you examine the rough draft. Ask yourself, as the recipient, whether you are able to comprehend the request quickly and if enough information has been included to enable a timely response.

Look for the obvious errors first. Check for spelling, sentence structure and grammar mistakes. Remember that a passive voice is not as commanding as an active one. You want your inquiry to be strong, so write with an active voice.

Keep in mind is the overall cohesiveness of the whole unit. Look for accuracy, clarity and a sense of completeness. Ask yourself if the transitions between paragraphs are working and if your point of view, tone and style are consistent throughout the text.

Examine your word choices carefully. Ambiguous words lead to confusion. Jargon and abstract terms may not be understood at all and affectations, clichés and trite language serve no real purpose and will obscure your objective. You want to help your reader understand exactly what it is that you want, so remove all that is not helpful.

And finally, if you have not written an opening or a conclusion now is the time. The introduction needs to lead into the body of your letter with a firm statement about the subject of your inquiry and enough supporting information to keep the reader reading. Your closing remarks need to reiterate your objective with a question that calls for an action.

Inquiry Letters

A letter of inquiry is a letter of request. The objective is to get the reader to respond with an action that satisfies the request. The action taken can benefit either the writer or the reader, and sometimes both. That being the case, the scope of an inquiry letter must include enough information to help the reader determine how best to respond.

In the sample inquiry letter there is a benefit to both the writer and the reader. In it the writer asks for some information and some help. It also makes an offer to the reader that provides an incentive to act.

Here are the steps to follow when writing an inquiry letter:

- Identify your reader.
- Establish your objective.
- Determine your scope.
- Organise your letter.
- Draft your letter
- Close Your letter
- Review and revise your letter

Identify Your Reader

An inquiry letter should be addressed to a specific person whenever possible. Doing so improves your odds on receiving a reply. Naming a person in your letter's salutation, and on the inside heading and envelope informs the reader that you have done your homework. It announces that you have identified them as being the likely contact person to whom you can direct your request, and to whom you can turn for help. Identifying your reader is not always possible, but often a quick phone call will do the job. Most businesses and organisations will supply names and contact procedures over the phone. It is especially important to check on procedures, as it is not unusual for large companies to have specific protocols for contacting their employees and associates. You will be expected to follow them.

Remember that people do business with people first, businesses second. Valuable time can be lost when an inquiry letter is sent to the wrong person or address. In the inside heading of the sample inquiry letter the reader is identified by both his name and the title he holds. In situations where you do not have the name of a contact person to address, consult the Formatting Business Letters page for acceptable options.

Establish Your Objective

The objective in an inquiry letter is communicated by one or more questions to which the writer desires a response. The question(s) will either ask the reader to provide something beneficial to the writer, or ask the reader to take advantage of a benefit that the writer has to offer.

Phrase your question(s) in a tone and style that is both courteous and straightforward. Be specific and brief. If you are asking for multiple pieces of information you might consider placing them into a bulleted list. This tactic acts like a snapshot highlighting the components of your objective. In the body of the sample inquiry letter, the writer states his objective by asking the reader for help in compiling information. He then outlines the scope of his needs in a bulleted list immediately following her request.

Answer the questions raised by the sample statements or build your own. You will end up with a list of things you want the reader to do or provide.

Determine Your Scope

The scope of an inquiry letter is contained in the information you provide for the specific purpose of helping the reader grasp your objective. You may safely assume that your reader is a busy person, so getting to the point is important. Your goal is to have the reader make a decision quickly and respond in a timely manner. Information that is not related to your objective should be left out.

Consider your targeted reader. Make it your business to now something about that person. What is their title or position? Are they the president of the company or the shipping clerk?

Do they have what you want? Can they do what you ask? Give them the relevant background information needed in order to make an informed decision. Let the reader know who you are and something about your motive. If you are to receive some benefit, it may help to explain for what purpose the benefit will be used. If the reader is to receive some benefit, it may help to offer an incentive to respond.

Put yourself in the reader's shoes and ask yourself what and how much background information is needed in order to take the action you are requesting. Would you already know everything you need to know, or would you need a little more? While you are in their shoes you might also ask yourself how much persuasion you would you need in order to be moved to act.

This will help you determine whether you have supplied too much information, or not enough. It will also help you determine what information needs to be qualified or amplified for the reader's benefit.

In the body of the sample inquiry letter the writer supplies relevant logistical information that the reader will need in order to respond quickly and effectively.

Make a list of relevant information that explains the reason for your inquiry. Think about what your reader will need to know before making a decision.

Organise Your Letter

Organising an inquiry letter is a simple procedure designed to help you draft your request. You have already started this task. You have established your objective and determined the scope of your inquiry. Refer back to them. Together they make up the main components in the body of your letter.

A simple outline will get you organised. A list will probably do the job. Consider each item on the list as having a logical place, either at the beginning, the middle or the end of your letter. Put each item where it belongs.

With list in hand you can begin a rough draft. Most of your thinking is done and you can concentrate on the writing task. You won't be worried about forgetting something important. It's already on your list. You won't be worried about in what order things should appear. Your list is already organised. When you begin the rough draft your outline will become a checklist.

Consult the points you have established in your objective and scope and decide where they belong. Are they part of the beginning, the middle or the end? Organise the information point by point in an order that makes sense. If it does not flow naturally, you may have something out of order. Feel free to move things around. On completion you will have a simple outline that can be saved and edited.

Draft Your Letter

Drafting an inquiry letter is a process by which your outline notes become sentences and paragraphs. Keep in mind; it's O.K. to be sloppy, you are writing a rough draft. Your spelling can be imperfect, your sentences can be grammatically incorrect and your paragraph structure can be less than impeccable. These things will be accounted for in the final step when you review and revise your work.

Write without fear. Your only concern is getting the point of your objective across to the reader and providing the relevant scope of information that supports your request. A draft will get it all down on paper. Best advice; be quick about it. Enlarge each sentence fragment in your outline until it expresses a complete thought. Gather your thoughts into paragraphs and then give yourself a rest. That's right-take a break. Do one at a time, starting with the point that you are most confident about turning into a complete sentence. Then do the others. Remember, it is best to do this quickly. On completion you will have a rough draft that can be saved and edited.

Close Your Letter

An inquiry letter should close with a professional tone and style. Once your last paragraph is written, sign off between a complimentary close such as "Sincerely" or "Thank you," and your printed name.

If your inquiry letter is written in conjunction with an official duty, place your title below the printed name as in the sample inquiry letter. Additional information such as dictation remarks, notification of attachments and copies sent to other individuals should be placed beneath your title line.

In situations where you are unsure of the proper close, consult the Formatting Business Letters page for acceptable options.

Review and Revise Your Letter

Reviewing and revising your inquiry letter is the final step in the writing process. You will check your draft in this step, making sure that your objective is clear and your scope is concise. Put yourself in the reader's shoes as you examine the rough draft. Ask yourself, as the recipient, whether you are able to comprehend the request quickly and if enough information has been included to enable a timely response.

Look for the obvious errors first. Check for spelling, sentence structure and grammar mistakes. Remember that a passive voice is not as commanding as an active one. You want your inquiry to be strong, so write with an active voice. The important thing to keep in mind is the overall cohesiveness of the whole unit. Look for accuracy, clarity and a sense of completeness. Ask yourself if the transitions between paragraphs are working and if your point of view, tone and style are consistent throughout the text.

Examine your word choices carefully. Ambiguous words lead to confusion. Jargon and abstract terms may not be understood at all and affectations, clichés and trite language serve no real purpose and will obscure your objective. You want to help your reader understand exactly what it is that you want, so remove all that is not helpful.

And finally, if you have not written an opening or a conclusion now is the time. The introduction needs to lead into the body of your letter with a firm statement about the subject of your inquiry and enough supporting information to keep the reader reading. Your closing remarks need to reiterate your objective with a question that calls for an action.

Response to an Inquiry Letter

When you receive an inquiry letter, answer the questions as clearly and as concisely as possible. If you cannot answer the questions, explain the reasons and offer to assist with alternate methods.

Order Letters

An order letter, also known as a PO (purchase order) begins the paper trail of a specific purchase. The objective is to provide detailed instructions to a vendor fulfilling an order. It is also serves as a legal document recording the transaction. It should be written with careful attention to detail.

Your intentions need to be clear and concise. The reader will fill your order only according to your instructions and your satisfaction will depend largely upon their accuracy.

The scope of an order letter should include only the information needed to fulfill the order. Keep in mind that in most cases the seller does not need to know why you are placing the order, what it is going to be used for or for whom it is intended. Such information is unnecessary when placing an order.

In the sample order letter the writer purchases three specific widgets from an out of date vendor catalogue. The reader can infer that either an infrequent customer or a new customer is placing the order.

- Identify your reader.
- Establish your objective.
- Determine your scope.
- Organise your letter.
- Draft your letter
- Close Your letter
- Review and revise your letter

Identify Your Reader

An order letter does not necessarily need a clearly identified reader. In fact, most first-time and one-time-only orders are just addressed to the attention of the Sales department within a company.

In these cases, the inside heading of the letter will contain just the name and address of the company to whom the order is being sent, and the salutation will be replaced by a simple attention getting device such as that shown in the sample order letter.

Establishing an account with a company will announce that your intention is to have an ongoing business relationship. At that time a specific contact person, to whom all future orders can be directed, will be assigned to handle your account. In situations where you do not have the name of a contact person to address, consult the Formatting Business Letters page for acceptable options.

Establish Your Objective

The objective of an order letter is to clearly indicate to the recipient that you are making a purchase. You should be brief. In the body of the sample order letter, the writer begins by saying that he is placing an order. He concludes his order with some specific instructions.

Determine Your Scope

The scope of an order letter should provide only that information relevant to accomplishing the objective of making a purchase: what the item is, the terms of the purchase and any specific shipping instructions. It provides the reader with an exact description of what is expected.

In the body of the sample order letter the writer has formatted his list of purchases in a table and provided a brief instruction linking his payment instructions to his shipping instructions. He has also included a phone number at which he can be reached should there be any difficulties fulfilling the order. Make a simple list of what you want to purchase. Be specific. Attention to detail is very important. Feel free to delete or add items. You can save and edit this list as you work. On completion you will have determined your scope.

Organise Your Letter

Organising a order letter is just a practical way to begin drafting a written notification of pending purchase. You have already started this task by establishing your objective and determining the scope. Refer back to them. Together they make up the main components in the body of your letter.

A simple outline will get you organised. Make a list of the things that your credit letter will include and put them in a sequential order that will best help your reader comprehend your response.

If the information does not flow naturally, you may have something out of order. Feel free to move things around. On completion you will have a simple outline.

Draft Your Letter

Working from an outline is the simplest way to draft a adjustment letter. Refer back to your list and turn each fragmentary sentence into a full and complete sentence expressing a single thought or idea.

Concentrate on communicating your objective to your reader. Be certain that you describe the scope of your solution with an appropriate amount of information.

Keep in mind that you are writing a rough draft. For an overall sense of cohesion, be as quick as you can. Spelling, grammar, sentence and paragraph structure need not be perfect. Those details will be tuned up in the final step when you review and revise your work.

Start with the point that you feel the strongest or most confident about and then do the others. Remember to do this quickly. On completion you will have a rough draft that can be saved and edited.

Do one at a time, starting with the point that you are most confident about turning into a complete sentence. Then do the others. Remember, it is best to do this quickly. On completion you will have a rough draft that can be saved and edited.

Close Your Letter

An order letter should close with a professional tone and style. Once your last paragraph is written, sign off between a complimentary close such as "Sincerely" or "Thank you," and your printed name.

If your order letter is written in conjunction with an official duty, place your title below the printed name as in the sample order letter. Additional information such as dictation remarks, notification of attachments and copies sent to other individuals should be placed beneath your title line.

In situations where you are unsure of the proper close, consult the Formatting Business Letters page for acceptable options.

Review and Revise Your Letter

Reviewing and revising your order letter is the final step in the writing process. You will check your draft in this step, making sure that your objective is clear and your scope is concise. Put yourself in the reader's shoes as you examine the rough draft. Ask yourself, as the recipient, whether you are able to comprehend the request quickly and if enough information has been included to enable a timely response.

Look for the obvious errors first. Check for spelling, sentence structure and grammar mistakes. Remember that a passive voice is not as commanding as an active one. You want your order to be strong, so write with an active voice.

The important thing to keep in mind is the overall cohesiveness of the whole unit. Look for accuracy, clarity and a sense of completeness. Ask yourself if the transitions between paragraphs are working and if your point of view, tone and style are consistent throughout the text.

Examine your word choices carefully. Ambiguous words lead to confusion. Jargon and abstract terms may not be understood at all and affectations, clichés and trite language serve no real purpose and will obscure your objective. You want to help your reader understand exactly what it is that you want, so remove all that is not helpful.

And finally, if you have not written an opening or a conclusion now is the time. The introduction should lead into the letter with a firm statement about the details of your order. The conclusion should reiterate your objective and, when appropriate, contain any explicit instructions.

This is the most common form of business communication, and it is written for a manufacturer, wholesaler, or retailer.

When writing an order letter, include all the information the reader will need to identify the merchandise, such as

- Quantity
- Model number
- Dimensions
- Capacity
- Material
- Price

As shown in the sample order letter, the actual details are formatted into a table bracketed by very short opening and closing paragraphs.

Sales Letter

When writing a sales letter, it is important to have a good attitude in order to sell your product or service, because the reader will want to know why they should spend their valuable time reading the letter. Therefore, you need to provide clear, specific information that will explain to the reader why they should be interested in buying your product or service.

Sales letters usually have a four-part strategy

- Catch the reader's eye: it is very crucial in a sales letter to attract the reader's attention or else you will probably fail to sell your product or service.
- Describe the product or service you are trying to sell.
- Convince your reader that your claims are accurate: back up your comments with research and facts.
- Give the reader opportunities to learn more about your product or service: provide the reader with a phone number, a Web site address, or some way for them to seek out information on their own.

SEVEN C'S OF BUSINESS LETTER WRITING

Effective letter writing boils down to knowing why you are writing a letter, understanding your reader's needs and then clearly writing what you need to say. Every letter should be clear, human, helpful and as friendly as the topic allows. The best letters have a conversational tone and read as if you were talking to your reader. In brief then, discover the Seven-C's of letter writing. You should be

- Clear
- Concise
- Correct
- Courteous
- Conversational

- Convincing
- Complete

When you write a letter, you are trying to convince someone to act or react in a positive way. Your reader will respond quickly only if your meaning is crystal clear.

Put yourself in the reader's shoes and write in a friendly and helpful tone. Don't represent your company as one that cannot make a mistake and must always be in the right. Try not to reply in the normal bland and defensive way of organisations—write a sincere and helpful letter.

Show you are interested in the reader's circumstances. If he or she has mentioned something personal in the letter, refer to it in your reply. This builds a bridge between you and the reader. Read the original letter carefully and see if there is something you can put in your letter to show your interest.

10

EFFECTIVE MEETING COMMUNICATION

Meetings are the most popular method of interactive communication. They facilitate direct, face-to-face communication and are essential at various levels in all organisations. They facilitate exchange of information, fostering of team spirit and commitment to common goals and objectives. More importantly, they help in elaborating ideas, clarifying concepts and clearing confusion, if any, created on account of ambiguous and incomplete verbal and vocal messages. Misunderstandings arising from unclear memos, circulars, directives, targets, etc. can be cleared through meetings with the people concerned.

While meetings, which are effective, contribute to decisionmaking and positive outcome, ill conceived and indifferently conducted meetings entail enormous waste of time, efforts and other resources. They may even lead to chaos and confusion. It would therefore be imperative to give attention to certain details while convening meetings. The preparation for an effective meeting starts well in advance and there is a lot that needs to be attended to on the day of the meeting, during the meeting and thereafter till the minutes are drawn up and sent.

NEED AND PURPOSE OF MEETING

1. To coordinate or arrange activities.
2. To report on some activity or experience.
3. To put forward ideas or grievances for discussion.
4. To give information to a group of people.
5. To obtain assistance.
6. To create involvement and interest.

TYPES OF MEETINGS

Formal Meetings

The rules of conduct of formal meetings are laid down in a company's Articles of Association and/or Constitution or Standing Orders. With such meetings a quorum must be present, i.e the minimum number of people who should be present in order to validate the meeting. A formal record of these meetings must be kept, usually by the company secretary.

Annual General Meeting (AGM)

AGM's are held once a year to assess the trading of the organisation over the year . All shareholders are invited to intend the GM but they must be given 21 days notice.

Statutory Meetings

Statutory meetings are called so that the directors and shareholders communicate and consider special reports. Companies are required by law to hold these statutory meetings.

Board Meetings

Board meetings are held as often as individual organisations require. They are attended by all directors and chaired by the Chairman of the board.

Informal Meetings

Informal meetings are not restricted by the same rules and regulation as formal meetings. Such meetings may take the form of brainstorming or discussion sessions where strict agendas may not be necessary and minutes may not be kept. However, it is usually considered good business practice for an agenda to be issued to all members prior to the meetings so that they can be prepare adequately in order to make a valuable contribution.

These meetings are attended by a group of managers who may need to discuss a specific matter, report of progress reports. For example the marketing manager, sales manager, production manager and research and development manager may meet to discuss the launch of a new product being launched soon.

BEFORE THE MEETING

Background Papers

Every meeting of some importance will have a set of background papers, which are sent in advance to the members who, will participate in the meeting. These background papers relate to the items listed in the agenda and provide glimpses of the issues involved. Background papers are normally prepared by the concerned functionaries or functional departments who are seeking a decision on the issue. Background papers cover all relevant details that are germane to effective deliberation and would normally include facts, figures, different views, expert opinion, latest position, and so on. Minutes of the previous meeting are also sent along with the first lot of background papers since it is always the first item on the agenda. They are also taken up for confirmation before proceeding to the other items.

Background papers ensure that deliberations are focused and cover all relevant dimensions of the subject under discussion.

Background papers should state clearly what is expected of the meeting. Board notes, office notes, etc. put up for important meetings should state clearly whether the note is submitted for "consideration and orders" or submitted for "information". It is also a common practice to state the "Resolution" covering the type of orders sought to ensure abundant clarity.

Whom to Invite

To be effective, deliberations at the meetings should involve all the concerned functionaries and persons. Regular members of the committees, wherever formally constituted, will have to be invariably invited. At the same time, in the absence of a formal list, it would be essential to identify people whose presence would be of significance when subjects are taken up for deliberation. In some cases, senior functionaries will have to - be necessarily invited to lend authority to the decision making process whereas some junior level functionaries and subject matter specialists may have to be present to provide technical details and other relevant backpapers. Persons to be invited for the meeting, wherever not specifically stated, are best decided in consultation with the chairperson and other senior functionaries on whose behalf the meeting is called.

Invitation for the meeting is to be clearly drawn up indicating the day, date, time and venue of the meeting. Invitations have to be sent well in advance to ensure that outstation participants have sufficient time to make appropriate travel plans. Meeting notices will have to clearly indicate who should attend the meeting. Sometimes, people in organisations receive notices, which do not clearly indicate whether they are sent as an invitation or just as intimation. The addressee in this case is likely to be confused and will have to start making further enquiries. The meeting notice should also state whether the addressee, if not in a position to attend, can depute someone else on his behalf. Though most of these are-simple necessaries, they are often overlooked.

Timing and Venue

Care should be taken in fixing up meetings in a manner that is generally convenient to most of the members or participants. A notice in advance will ensure that participants get adequate opportunity to schedule or reschedule their engagements. The date and time should be fixed taking into account holidays, other important events and functions that may clash with meeting timings and make it difficult for the members to choose between one or the other. While it may not be possible to totally avoid overlapping in all cases, some advance planning and enquiries will certainly help better attendance at meetings. Indication of the duration of the meeting will also be helpful so that the participants would know how much time is to be allocated for it. Also, details such as arrangements for breakfast, lunch, etc. need to be mentioned.

While reasonable advance intimation for any meeting facilitates better attendance, any notice sent months in advance or much earlier will have to be necessarily followed up with subsequent reminders.

The venue of the meeting should be fixed up obviously well before the meeting notices are dispatched. With so many meetings taking place there is bound to be considerable demand for meeting halls and conference rooms. The meeting room should have all the physical facilities - fans, air conditioners, microphones, projectors, etc. that ensure minimum comfort for the members and facilitate uninterrupted deliberations. Physical barriers such as non— availability of sound systems, extraneous sounds, cramped seating, etc. hinders effective communication. It is not uncommon in organisations to come across instances where the availability of venue is not confirmed or there is some misunderstanding in the date or time as a result of which either meeting are delayed or participants are made to move from one venue to another. A little extra care will avoid much embarrassment at the time of meeting.

There are occasions when the chief executive or other senior functionary may decide to convene impromptu or emergent meetings with very short notice in which case the availability of venue, physical facilities and other arrangements for refreshments, etc. will have to be attended to on priority: A situation where the deliberations have concluded and yet refreshments or lunch is not ready speaks of poor preparations and has to be scrupulously avoided. Also the participants' time is important and cannot be taken for granted.

Punctuality

Starting the meeting on time is an area that calls for conscious efforts. Keeping the venue open, reminding the Chairman and other members, ensuring that all papers have reached the participants, and table items are placed, and ensuring that the convenors and organisers are at the venue well before the scheduled time are all a must in making meetings time bound and purposeful. A situation where the convenor is still in consultation with the chairman of the meeting, well past the scheduled starting time, while the participants' are waiting in the venue not knowing when and if at all the meeting would take place is the kind of situation that speaks of the indifferent attitude towards the meeting and must be avoided.

Time Management

Time management is of essence in ensuring the effectiveness of meetings. Meetings, which start on time, end on time and provide adequate time for proper deliberation of all listed items, ensure cost effectiveness. On the contrary, meetings that start with undue delay, take up items not on priority and run out of focus entail waste of efforts and time and prove to be costly to the organisation. On_ tan "assess the efficiency level of an organisation in terms of effectiveness of the meetings conducted at various levels.

Checklist for Meetings

The convenor or the secretariat for the meetings will have to take responsibility for the success of the meetings. They have to invariably give attention to details and ensure that everything is in order. It would be desirable to maintain a checklist of items to be checked at various stages Le., before, during and after the meeting.

The checklist should include, among others, the following items:

- Venue arrangements such as ensuring that the meeting hall is ready and open well in time, checking whether all equipments such as mikes, air conditioners, fans, projectors are functioning, providing pens and pads, etc.
- Refreshments and catering as are appropriate to the meeting.
- Checking flight arrivals, room bookings, conveyance, etc. for chairperson and others wherever required.
- Reminding the local members about the time and venue of the meeting.

- Ensuring that all relevant background papers have reached the members as intended'.
- Ascertaining the participation of members and the availability of quorum Ensuring that table items required for the day's meeting are put up.
- Briefing the chairman and other key members about the issues to be taken up in the meeting.
- Entrustment of responsibility concerning the recording of minutes or proceedings.
- Preparation of minutes on time, obtaining approval for the same and their dispatch.
- Timely intimation of postponement, cancellation, change of venue, etc.
- Changes to be effected in the composition of the members or participants, special invitees, etc.
- This kind of attention to all details by the convenor or the secretariat brings in the much-needed professional approach in conducting meetings.

Role of the Chairperson

The Chairperson, the convenor or the secretary and senior members have a vital role to play in conducting the meetings effectively. He or she has to ensure punctuality and effective time management. While providing the freedom for expressing views on items taken up for deliberation, the chairperson ensures that discussions do not stray.

The Chairperson ensures that as far as possible, all the agenda items slated for discussion are duly taken up for deliberation. The chairperson may also have to make appropriate opening remarks and concluding remarks in the interest of directing deliberations and arriving at clear decisions. Through his experience, wit and wisdom, he brings in authority and decisiveness to the deliberations.

If, during the course of deliberations, members get into a war of words, or personal clash, the chairperson will have to use his or her skill in resolving such conflicts without hurting the people concerned. When meetings are either long or very frequent, some time may have to be spent in warming up or refreshing the participants or what may be called unwinding. Participants in all the meetings are the people and people management will have to be done smoothly. It is common fact that sometimes discussions in meetings tend to revolve too much on insignificant or irrelevant topics, leaving much less time for deliberating on the most important topics. The chairperson or the convenor who should play a complementary role in conducting the meetings, should intervene and bring in the much needed sense of proportion.

To conclude, it should be reiterated that meetings, when conducted effectively, could bring in substantial benefits in resolving even sensitive matters through collective wisdom. They can be very cost effective means of intensive interaction. When participants learn to talk, listen and interact in a responsible manner, meetings can be really result-oriented. At the same time, it should be borne in mind that although the people participating are knowledgeable, they mayor may not speak out freely and contribute to the deliberations. Sometimes, some of the participants may tend to dominate the deliberations, not giving an opportunity to others to express themselves. In other words, it takes conscious efforts and attention to details in ensuring that meetings are effective.

MEETING PROCEDURES

For success of the problem-solving meeting, the leader's attitude and efficiency-from the beginning statement through the entire discussion are critically important. The leader should be well prepared, be able to think and act quickly, get along with others, respect their opinions, know objectives of discussion and the reasoning process, be patient, and have a sincere interest in the values of cooperative group action. This section lists procedures the leader should follow in conducting the meeting:

1. *Begin with appropriate opening statement:* Obviously, you should prepare your introductory statement before the meeting but neither memorise nor read it. Present it informally and naturally-in one or more of these suggested ways:

   Good morning/ afternoon, everyone.

   If we are all here, let's.:.

   . . . .get started

   . . . .start the meeting.

   .. . .start.

   Other possibilities are open to you as chairperson, but the above are some of the most common.

2. *Stimulate discussion for solution discovery*: In general, try to encourage all member's to participate, and do keep the discussion moving forward. To help spark discussion on each topic, ask questions and keep participants from wandering onto irrelevant paths. Sometimes if the original contributor of an idea cannot add to it, another member may be able to carry it further. If a participant's statement is vague, rephrase it clearly. Maintain an atmosphere of goodwill and cooperation throughout the meeting. If a situation becomes tense or some members are reluctant to speak or are annoying or antagonistic, try to calm down the situation. Even taking a recess diffuses tensions. Try to be tactful, considerate, and understanding and show a sense of humour.

3. *Understand roles of participants:* In a meeting, different participants (including the chairperson) tend to acquire some roles. These roles may be categorised as task roles — roles facilitating the achievement of the task assigned to the meeting, and group building and maintenance roles — roles facilitating the harmony in the meeting so that meeting goes undisturbed. While performing a task role, an individual may play as coordinator, or information seeker, or opinion seeker, or information giver, or opinion giver, or recorder. While playing the group building and maintenance role, an individual may perform as encourager, compromiser, follower, and likewise. Knowing the various roles being played by group members assists the leader in knowing how to react, how to handle role statements made during a meeting.
4. Particularly important, however, is handling a problem participant
   — Here are some suggestions for leaders on handling difficult members:

   (a) *The quiet, non-participating member:* First ask this person question he can answer by a simple "yes" or "no". Then, whenever possible, ask this member to give some information that he is sure to know because of job, training, or experience. Thank and praise the person as much as you can; he may then be more likely to enter the discussion confidently.

   (b) *The "know-it-all-":* This person may be asked to justify every statement he or she makes. Whenever possible, ask other members for their opinions of these statements. Sometimes, it necessary and you feel the majority are annoyed by this person's arrogance, you may tactfully quiet the person by asking for a show of hands from the group, which strongly outvotes the know-it-all's suggestions. If the negative member still insists on knowing all the answers, a private, outside-the-meeting session can bring the group's concern to the person. This one-on-one meeting in a non-threatening atmosphere may produce more positive results.

(c) *The long-winded speaker:* You may thank this excessive talker when he is at the end of a sentence, and then recognise someone else. Or you might move the discussion to another highly important point, perhaps with a statement like "Well, we have two more points, perhaps with a statement like "Well, we have two more points to consider before we wind up this meeting, so let's move along to the next topic.

(d) *The erroneous member:* If the other members—out of respect-are reluctant to correct this person, an especially tactful comment by you, the leader, may be required. As with any bad-news message, avoid direct criticism, sarcasm, or ridicule. Shield the person's pride. When praising people, single them out; when criticising them, put them in a group. Perhaps analyse a similar case, without referring to the speaker personally.

(e) *The member who shows personal animosity:* Though rare, sometimes an angry member shouts hateful, tactless comments towards another member or members. You can show an attitude of calm understanding and turn him or her of by directing a question to another member.

5. *Sort, select, interpret data for solution evaluation:* After you have listed members' suggestions on the board, encourage participants to consider advantages and disadvantages of each suggested course of action. List them separately. As leader, be careful not to impose your own opinions on the group, or if you wish to participate, ask another member to chair the meeting. Encourage each group member to feel a sense of responsibility for the success of the analysis. Good listening by everyone to what others offer is extremely important.
6. *State the conclusion and plan of action:* As with a written analytical report, the terminal section is of major importance. Before you dismiss the meeting, review what the group has accomplished. Summarise what parts of the problem members have solved or partially solved. State the decision clearly and definitely. You might begin your statement of the conclusion by saying "You have agreed.. .."or "You have suggested.. ..." or It's my interpretation that we have approved" rather than. "I think this is what should be done." If the group arrived at several conclusions, list them, preferably in order to importance. Make some statement about how the solution the group decided on will be carried out. Appointments may be made then or announced later in a memo regarding the action.
7. *Follow-up after the meeting:* Two functions after the meeting are distribution of the minutes and-most important-seeing that responsible committees, departments, or individuals are appointed to carry out the chosen action. In some situations the meeting leader may have to confer with other executives of higher authority before appointments are made regarding policy decisions.

Copies of the minutes your secretary or assistant prepared should be sent to the meeting participants soon after the meeting.

They usually should include:

- Name of the organisation, department, or group
- Date, time, place of the meeting
- Names of members present
- Names of any others present as invited visitors
- Name of chairperson and recording secretary
- Brief summary of reports, if any, by those listed on the agenda
- Highlights of solutions presented and decisions made Time of adjournment and date or next meeting.

As follow-up, e-mail an attachment of the meeting notes to each of the participants. Or save them to the company's network in a meetings folder. This way, all the meeting participants have access to the meeting notes if there's an idea or discussion they'd like to revisit. In the e-mail, also summarise the action items assigned during the meeting. Outline what was assigned, to whom it was assigned, the priority level and the due date. When a meeting's adjourned, it's not always clear who's responsible for what, which means action items aren't always carried through. By summarising the action items in an e-mail, you can be certain all participants understand who's responsible for what.

TIPS FOR EFFECTIVE MEETINGS

Don't Meet

Avoid a meeting if the same information could be covered in a memo, e-mail or brief report. One of the keys to having more effective meetings is differentiating between the need for one-way information dissemination and two-way information sharing.

Set Objectives for the Meeting

Set objectives before the meeting! Before planning the agenda for the meeting, write down a phrase or several phrases to complete the sentence: By the end of the meeting, I want the group to... Depending on the focus of your meeting, your ending to the sentence might include phrases such as: ...be able to list the top three features of our newest product, ...have generated three ideas for increasing our sales, ...understand the way we do business with customers, ...leave with an action plan, ...decide on a new widget supplier, or ...solve the design problem.

Provide an Agenda Beforehand

Provide all participants with an agenda before the meeting starts. Your agenda needs to include a brief description of the meeting objectives, a list of the topics to be covered and a list stating who will address each topic and for how long.

Assign Meeting Preparation

Give all participants something to prepare for the meeting, and that meeting will take on a new significance to each group member. For problem-solving meetings, have the group read the background information necessary to get down to business in the meeting. Ask each group member to think of one possible solution to the problem to get everyone thinking about the meeting topic.

Assign Action Items

Don't finish any discussion in the meeting without

deciding how to act on it. Listen for key comments that flag potential action items and don't let them pass by without addressing them during your meeting. Statements such as We should really... that's a topic for a different meeting... or I wonder if we could... are examples of comments that should trigger action items to get a task done, hold another meeting or further examine a particular idea.

Examine your Meeting Process

Assign the last few minutes of every meeting as time to review the following questions: What worked well in this meeting? What can we do to improve our next meeting? Every participant should briefly provide a point-form answer to these questions. Answers to the second question should be phrased in the form of a suggested action. For example, if a participant's answer is stated as Jim was too longwinded, ask the participant to rephrase the comment as an action. The statement We should be more to-the-point when stating our opinions is a more constructive suggestion. Remember – don't leave the meeting without assessing what took place and making a plan to improve the next meeting!